Guideposts

---

for growing up

by ELIZABETH B. HURLOCK, *Ph.D.*

Associate in Psychology,
The Graduate School
University of Pennsylvania

1974

Standard Educational Corporation

Chicago

*Grateful acknowledgment is made
to William Nicoll for the typography,
and to Donald G. Wheeler for the illustrations.*

Dear parents

Sometimes I feel a bit envious of the people who write books with such titles as "How to Raise Turkeys" and "The Care and Feeding of Horses." These writers, it seems to me, have an easy job. They can give long lists of rules and instructions, and very few will argue over their advice.

What a different story when we deal with laughing, crying, growing boys and girls! First of all, it's so much easier to learn all about a chicken or a cow than it is to learn about a child. And who would dare write a list of rules and regulations and say they fit all children everywhere? Who would honestly claim to know all there is to know about the rearing of children?

As a matter of fact, a good deal of progress *has* been made in the field of child guidance. Today, much is known about children that our own fathers and mothers did not know—and even more that *their* parents did not know. Through careful observation of many children, painstaking research, checking and cross-checking facts gathered on normal as well as handicapped children, there has been built up a growing body of reliable information on childhood and parenthood.

As mother, teacher, and researcher, it has been my good fortune to keep in closest touch with this scientific study of childhood. Now, in this book, I am happy to share with you the important information and useful ideas that can help make your job as parents even more rewarding and joyful.

Elizabeth B. Hurlock

Contents

chapter 1

Your child
is an individual

Y<small>OUR</small> child is different from every other child. Johnnie, Charles, Sue, or Betty—each one is an *individual* in his own right. Each has a special body build, a different rate of growth, a style of behavior that is his very own.

We can see these differences even in a group of babies. One is frail, another stocky. This one is active and bubbling over with energy; that one is placid and slow-moving. And as each infant grows into childhood, we can see these differences more clearly. Here's Patty, who tries and tries until she manages to tie a bow, but there's Lucy, who gives up very quickly. Tommy is always smiling and even-tempered, but Wally is jumpy and overly sensitive.

Every child is special

Respect should start early

P<small>ERHAPS</small> *the most important thing that we, as parents, can do in rearing a child is to keep these differences in mind.* Recognize and respect your son's or daughter's individuality from

7

the moment he or she is born. As time goes on, your child will develop according to his own traits and capacities. He will be different from other children because of these individual potentialities. At home, in school, on the playground—encourage these differences. Don't scorn them, for they do not mean he is inferior.

A child needs opportunities

And you can't expect a child to develop into the kind of person mother or father *would have liked to become* if only life had turned out just a bit different! Even in early life, a child must be given opportunities to try his own powers, his own inclinations. He needs to be helped and guided to understand those powers and inclinations. And he needs help in learning how to make the most of them. To give him the most intelligent and helpful guidance, we must understand how a child grows.

A child is not a miniature adult

Have you noticed that a little child has a top-heavy appearance? That's because the head develops faster than the rest of a child's body. His muscular strength, his endurance, the functioning of his internal organs—all are in a state of growth. Physically, the child is still immature.

This is true psychologically, too. He is still growing mentally. He hasn't lived long enough to learn adult ways of doing things or of looking at life's problems. Because of his inexperience, he's immature in his approach to people and situations.

What to expect

It is true that a child will carry over into adulthood many of the physical and psychological traits of his childhood. But these will change their form and their general appearance as he grows up. His skin and hair darken with age; his features change; his body shape alters. And the pouting, demanding 3-year-old often develops into a poised, cooperative teen-ager not at all like the "bratty" toddler!

So it isn't fair to expect adult behavior from a child. If you criticize him when he acts his age, he will be too discouraged to try to do what he is capable of doing. Don't expect too much. But don't expect too little, either, or he won't have an urge to live up to his capacities.

In the growing-up process, there will be times when his individuality will prove to be troublesome, I know. But that's no reason for trying to curb it. You want your child to have a well-rounded, wholesome personality that will make him happy and successful as he moves through life. Then help him mold his individuality into a pattern that can be an asset. You can do that by thinking of Johnny or Mary not as a "typical" 3-year-old or 6-year-old, but as Johnny Smith, an individual, or Mary Brown, an individual. You see, if you start thinking of a child as "typical," you will find it hard to recognize him as an individual.

Children are individuals

What every child needs

IF WE are to encourage every child to be an individual, how can we say what the *particular* needs of any one child will be? We can't, of course. But there are certain needs that are so *universal* that we *can* say they are typical of every child at every age—if he is to become a real person in his own right. Every child, I believe, needs—

1. Love, and expressions of love—not by kissing and fondling alone, but by words of appreciation and comfort.

2. Recognition of his achievements, no matter how poor they may be.

3. Security of home, and people to be with him.

4. Encouragement when he feels inadequate to meet a situation or problem.

5. Help in learning to be independent.

6. Confidence of others in his abilities to do the things he wants to do.

12 needs common to all children

7. Stimulating experiences and opportunities to develop · his inborn traits.

8. Playmates who are congenial.

9. Some place he can call his own, even if it is only part of a room shared with others.

10. Some possessions of his own, no matter how few; clothes, toys, books, even a pet.

11. Some time for himself—in the morning, afternoon, and before going to bed—to use in any way that *he* wants.

12. Some special responsibility to his family—a job *he* has selected because he can do it well and because it is useful to the family and will be appreciated *as his alone*.

Upset by children

*It bothers me the way my children behave when I take them out.
After I speak crossly to them or punish them, I realize they
are only children and that I cannot expect them to behave like grownups. How seriously does my annoyance affect the children?*

Y̲OUR children cannot understand why you are cross and upset when they behave in a manner which, *to them*, seems perfectly normal. They wonder why
you are cross with them and they probably take your reproofs as a sign you
don't love them.

Because they are still young, chances are they will forget single instances of
your annoyance. However, they are building up the general impression that you
do not understand or love them, and that you do not approve of them. In time—
if you do not learn to control your emotional upsets and angry outbursts—you will
build up in them doubt about their ability to do the right thing, and resentment
toward you. This will seriously hurt their personalities and their relationships
with you.

Individuality

*My son seems to delight in being different from the other children of
the neighborhood. Is this a good trait to encourage?*

A̲LL OF US know a child or an adult who delights in being different. What we
sometimes overlook is that such a "rugged individualist" is *not sure of himself*.
He is trying to make up for his doubts by taking on the attitude of "I'll show
them!" toward others. Of course, people will not stand for too much of this showing off. Therefore, it most certainly is not a desirable trait to cultivate. And yet,
within reason, it is wise to encourage your child to develop along the lines of his
own interests and capacities. It is wise to do this even if his interests do differ
from those of the children in his school and in the neighborhood.

Is this contradictory? No, not really. Take the child who is extremely bright.
He rarely enjoys the same play that children of his age, but of lower intelligence,
enjoy. He likes to read, to play games requiring mental activity, and to see movies
of a more mature sort than those enjoyed by other children his age. Or take the
child with musical talent. He will spend more of his leisure time listening to
music or playing an instrument than will a child more talented in woodwork or
in other manual work.

Our job is to encourage these children to develop their *own* talents. We don't
want to force them to do just what everyone else does. But there is another part
to our job, too: We must help them to understand and to respect *other* children's

interests and activities—even though they may have little in common with them. We want to keep them from developing the attitude of "I'm better than you."

Actually, this seldom becomes a real problem because few children have such one-sided abilities. Most children who are at the same level of development are basically alike in their interests and abilities. Where there *are* noticeable differences, children can still learn to do things they enjoy and, at the same time, get along well with other people.

Personality differences

My two children are just as different in personality as they are in looks. David is friendly and helpful but Michael seems to have a chip on his shoulder. He snubs our attempts to be affectionate with him. My husband and I try to treat both boys alike, so I don't know why they should be so different.

No MATTER how hard parents may try to treat their children alike, *they rarely succeed*. That's because it is natural for us to react to people according to *their* attitudes and behavior.

Let's take your own case. To friendly, outgoing David you probably are cheerful, kind, demonstrative. But what about Michael? When *he* is grumpy and disagreeable, refuses to cooperate, and perhaps even complains that you don't treat him fair, *you* may feel annoyed and make sharp, critical comments. Under those circumstances you are not likely to *show* him affection even though you may *feel* affection for him. Now this, in turn, reacts on *him*. It makes even stronger in him the belief he already has—the belief that no one loves him, that the world is against him.

I'm sure that when it comes to giving food, clothing, gifts, education, recreation, and other material things, you are fair to both David and Michael. But what about those other things that are so important for your children's personality development—your own attitudes and reactions toward your children? Here, whether you realize it or not, is probably where you are not treating both boys alike. And that is why you find such marked personality differences in the two.

There is another side to your problem, too. These different patterns of behavior that Michael and David have developed in the home lead them to act in different ways to people *outside* the home. Cheerful, affectionate David is doubtless more popular than grouchy Michael. Surely Michael has realized this, and that fact deepens even more the unpleasant personality pattern he is developing. What can you *do* about this situation? Try to change this pattern *before it is too late*. Bend over backwards to show Michael that you *do* love him, that you *do* want him to be happy. In your actions, show him that you are *for* him, not against him. In time this treatment should do away with his resentments and help Michael turn into a child similar to David.

11

Only child

Our daughter is our only child and the doctor tells me I must have no more children. Is it bad for a child to be an only child?

THAT depends on the parents. It is bad for a child to be an only child *only if the parents make it so!* The mere fact that a boy or girl is an only child is certainly not bad. This is proved by recent studies that compared only children with children who had brothers and sisters. Both groups were found to be about equally well-adjusted and popular. This difference was found: only children are more likely to be leaders than are children with brothers and sisters. This is because they are often more mature in their ways, due to their association with adults. (Of course, some only children are immature because they are babied and not given a chance to "act their age.")

It is true that there are some traits that people often claim to be typical of an only child: selfishness, dependency, uncooperativeness. But you and your husband can help your child avoid developing such undesirable qualities. Here are some suggestions: Never feel that your daughter is the center of your world. Don't allow her to do exactly as she pleases just because she has no playmates in the home. Treat her the same way you would if she had brothers and sisters. *Don't* close your eyes to faults she may have; *do* try to correct them. And encourage her to stand on her own feet.

Clothes

I have always tried to get individual clothes for my son and daughter. Now that they are in school, they want their clothes to be like the other children's. I hate to see my children looking like every other child, still, I do not want them to be unhappy.

A CHILD does not want to be different from other children in appearance or in anything else. There is nothing that will upset him and make him unhappy more quickly than to have to wear clothes that make him stand out from the group. By the time your children reach the late teens, they will be only too glad to have individual styles in their clothes.

In the future, consult them about the clothes you buy for them and be guided by their wishes. So long as the clothing is not going to injure their health, let them wear what they want, because that will be what the other children are wearing. You may feel that your daughter is not the type to wear ruffles and that she would look much better in tailored lines. But if her friends all wear ruffles, she will want to wear ruffles, too, even if they make her look like the side of a house. A child must be given opportunities to express his individuality—but in the area of clothing, this is not what he wants. Being like his friends in appearance is one way he identifies himself with them and gains security. So don't interfere with this very necessary prop to your children's security.

Parent ambitions

My husband wants our son to be an athlete, a good student, and an all-around success. Peter is in the first grade. His teacher says he has trouble with his work and that he doesn't get along well with the other children. Peter is a rather frail child. I am afraid he is going to be a great disappointment to his father.

THERE is nothing more unfair to a child than trying to force him into a parent's mold without considering the child's own abilities, interests, and ambitions. Peter will soon sense that father is disappointed in him. This will make Peter very resentful toward your husband. It will also build up in Peter a strong feeling that he is inferior to other children.

Try to convince your husband that he must accept your son *as he is* and love him *for what he is*. Your husband must do this even if the child is not what he has always dreamed he would like his son to be. Your husband may not realize that in his ambitions for Peter he is really trying to fulfill ambitions he himself was not able to achieve. He wants his son to do things which he himself always wanted to do but couldn't. *Help your husband see the selfishness of this.* Help him check his selfishness, quickly and completely. If he doesn't, Peter's personality will suffer.

chapter 2

Stages in growing up

Every child grows in stages, by spurts and stops, not in an even way. At some times, little Steve's *physical* growth is rapid while his *mental* growth seems to be at a resting point. At other times, his physical growth slows down and his mental development spurts ahead. His growth pattern, in other words, is rhythmic, not regular.

The growth pattern

This is typical of every child. All children follow this same *general* pattern of growing up. But—and this is important—no two children follow that pattern in exactly the same way. Each child varies in some respects from all other children. That is why no one can predict just what Steve will be able to do at 1 year, or at 5.

Bright versus dull

Of course, knowing something about the normal pattern of growth will help. You will be able to tell, in a general way, what a child will be able to do at a certain age. But you just cannot be sure that any one Steve or Mary or Harold or Susan will follow this pattern to the very letter.

Suppose Billie is ahead of Harold in certain areas of his development. Perhaps he begins to stand sooner, or to talk earlier. Does this mean that Billie is brighter than the other child? Not necessarily. It simply means that he is following his own pattern of growth. In this particular area of his development—standing, or talking—he is accelerated. It is only when a child is ahead of other children in almost *every* area of his development that we can safely conclude that he is "bright."

When is a child bright or dull?

If Harold, on the other hand, lags behind in talking or walking, this is not foolproof evidence that Harold is dull. It may just mean that he has not had the opportunity to develop in these areas. The cause may be poor health, or too few opportunities to get the necessary practice for learning. But if the child is lagging behind other children in *most* areas of his behavior, parents may have good reason to worry and wonder if their child is "normal." A complete physical and mental check-up by a doctor and a psychologist will quickly give the answer.

Because boys and girls develop at different rates, you cannot compare boys with girls. In some areas of their development, girls are ahead of boys. In other areas, the reverse is true.

Sex and rate of development

Likewise, *the child's position in the family* plays an important role in setting the rate and pattern of his development. First-born children are usually slower in developing than are second- or third-born. This is not because the first-born are weaker or duller than their younger brothers and sisters. Rather, it is because their parents generally have more time to do things *for them* than they have for the other children that follow. As a result, the first-born child has fewer chances to develop skills, and less incentive to do so, than if he had been born second or third in the family.

Every stage has its problems

For every stage of development there are problem forms of behavior that are usually found in children at that stage. These problems generally arise from the child's attempts to adjust to new and more complicated situations than he had to face before. Until the adjustment is complete, he is likely to do many things which his parents will label "problems."

Take the matter of dawdling over meals. The 2-year-old is not as hungry as he was during the first year of life, when he was growing by leaps and bounds. Now his growth is slowing down and his food needs are lessened. Furthermore, his active mind serves as a distracting influence. He sees so many things around him that are more interesting than food! So he leaves the table to examine them, he listens intently to what people are saying and forgets to eat, or he asks endless questions. While all this goes on, his food remains untouched, cold, uninviting. This kills what little interest he had in it, and the result is that he spends an unlimited time just sitting at the table, without eating.

The why of dawdling over meals

Your attitude toward these problems

How you deal with these adjustment problems will determine whether they will be temporary or lasting. Sometimes parents pay too much attention to them. Sometimes parents try to correct them before they have outlived their usefulness to the child. And sometimes parents take an intolerant attitude. All these ways are likely to turn these problems into serious ones that will be hard to overcome.

Being calm will help

It is not enough for parents to *understand* what lies back of these troublesome forms of behavior that crop up at every stage of growing up. They must go one step further and be *tolerant* of them. True, few parents *like* this troublesome behavior. But they must accept it calmly, realizing that it is part and parcel of the whole pattern of growing up.

"This too will pass" is a good motto for every parent to master. When your child seems especially annoying, remember: This too will pass. It will help calm any doubts you may have about the future behavior of your child. And it will help you take the behavior in stride while it lasts. You will skip some of the things parents often do in trying to root out troublesome behavior, things which often make matters worse instead of better.

A time table of development

WE HAVE seen that children do not develop in exactly the same way. Still, we can learn a good deal from the *typical pattern* of development that is based on studies of thousands of children.

Follow your child's growth, noting the changes he goes through from one age to another. As you do this, you will see how close he comes to this pattern—not so much in actual timing as in the *order* in which the different traits appear. A child does not *skip* a stage. The stage may be delayed or speeded up, or it may be in a form so mild that you barely recognize it. The main thing is that it will come some time, and the nearer it comes to the normal age, the better. When you see that the child's behavior is changing from the pattern you have noticed before, you will have a clue that he is ready to enter a higher stage in the pattern of development.

Order of changes in children

To give you some clues as to what to expect of your child at different ages, here is a "developmental time table" that should be useful. Use it with caution: don't become disturbed if your child does not follow it to the letter! Remember that no two children are alike. That is why it is impossible to make up a time table that would fit every child. Your child will, however, follow the general pattern of this chart at about the ages shown.

GROWTH FROM BIRTH TO ONE YEAR

Sleeps less each month, and for longer periods.
Eats less frequently and larger quantities each month.
Begins to take solids at third month, taking food from spoon.
Starts to chew on zwieback or toast by fourth month.
Drinks from cup at seventh month.
Tries to feed himself with spoon by tenth month.
Tries to hold cup by eleventh month.
Enjoys bath, plays with water toys and splashes water.
Begins to show a regular pattern for elimination.
Babbles and tries to imitate sounds.
Restless when tired, very fretful when excited.
Sits up first around sixth month.
Pulls himself to standing position by ninth month.
Starts to walk, holding on, between eleventh and twelfth months.
Explores body and everything he can get in his hands.
Cries frequently due to physical needs and, later, to get attention.

The first year

Troublesome traits

Fretful and whiny, especially when teeth are erupting.
Bangs head against crib, chews clothing and thumb.
Protests when dressed.
Pulls off cap, mittens, booties, and shoes.
Throws toys out of crib, play pen, or carriage.
Protests when left alone for any length of time.
Refuses many foods, especially when different.

Special needs

Regular schedule.
Familiar feeling of being handled by same persons.
Cuddling, affection, and expressions of love.
Calm environment.
Few visitors.
Opportunity to learn to amuse himself.

GROWTH FROM ONE TO TWO YEARS

Sleeps less, and wakens less easily.
Eats less and is often fussy about food.
Tries to feed himself, gradually learns to handle spoon.
Drinks from cup with little spilling.
Enjoys bath and tries to bathe himself.
Plays with simple toys, mostly by exploring them.
Enjoys being with adults, demands their attention.

The second year
Enjoys being with other children but spends time exploring them.
Tries to imitate words he hears and combines them in sentences.
Explores everything he can get hold of.
Asks endless questions.
Rebels against being left alone or in play pen.
Frightened of large animals, loud noises, or things and people who come upon him suddenly.
Tries to put on some of his clothes.
Shows resentment if too long a time is taken for dressing.
Is trained to use the toidy seat.
Keeps dry most of the time and rarely soils himself.

Becomes angry when activities are interfered with.
Demands much attention from parents and anyone around.
Wants to be with people most of the time.

Is into everything.
Destructive because of poor muscular control.
Dawdles over meals and refuses to eat foods he dislikes.
Shy with strangers.
Fretful and whiny when tired.

Help in learning how to do things for himself.
Plenty of opportunity to do things for himself.
Appreciation for his achievements, no matter how poor
they are.
Playtime with grownups where he gets their undivided
attention.
Plenty of demonstrations of affection from others.
Firmness, in rules, but kindness and understanding of his
shortcomings.

GROWTH FROM TWO TO FOUR YEARS

Always on the go, and prefers running to walking.
Is into everything but breaks less than formerly, because
of better muscular coordination.
Toilet trained, except for occasional "accidents" due to
excitement or fatigue.
Takes over responsibility for most of his bath.
Can put on all clothes, may need help with fasteners.
Feeds himself except for cutting some meats.
Dawdles over meal, either to get help in feeding or be-
cause he does not like the food.
Rebels at naps and dawdles over preparations for bed at
night.
Speaks in long, rambling sentences, often making gram-
matical errors.

From 2 to 4

Asks questions endlessly, mainly out of curiosity but sometimes to attract attention to himself.

Plays with toys by making things, dramatizing scenes, and by taking them apart.

Enjoys listening to stories, music, and watching television.

Plays simple games such as tag and hide-and-seek, preferably with adults.

Enjoys being with children but plays little and quarrels much with them.

Has frequent temper tantrums, especially when he cannot have his own way.

Shows affection for adults and pets.

Jealous of younger sisters or brothers, and shows it by trying to hurt them or to get more attention from mother.

Curious about religion and sex.

Troublesome traits

Temper outbursts, with kicking, biting, screaming, and throwing things.

Assertion of independence by saying "No" constantly to everything he is asked to do.

Jealousy of other children, and constant demands for attention.

Quarreling with other children in play.

Teasing pets and hurting them.

Dawdling over things he does not like to do.

Untidiness about his possessions and appearance.

Special needs

Plenty of play space, both indoors and out.

Supervision when playing with other children, to learn how to play with them.

Help in learning how to play with his toys.

Help in learning how to do things for himself.

Knowledge that someone will be available when he needs help.

Sympathy when he is sick or hurt.

Understanding of his need for independence.

Expressions of love even when he is naughty.

GROWTH FROM FOUR TO SIX YEARS

Rapid improvement in muscular movements.

Rapid learning of new play and self-help skills.

Always on the go, running and playing.

Rebels against mid-day rests, dawdles at bedtime.

Dresses himself completely, even tries to fix hair.

Takes own bath and tries to shampoo hair.

Has more interest in imaginative play and making things than in any other uses of toys.

Plays with other children in toy play.

Begins to take a real interest in clothes, especially when they are new or admired by others.

Likes to roller skate, climb fences, explore the neighborhood, and go on excursions to new places.

From 4 to 6

Enjoys rhythm in music and dancing.

Speech improves greatly if errors are corrected.

Wants to be read to, tries to identify words in books, and likes to look at pictures.

Enjoys television and radio programs for children.

Interested in Bible stories, likes to go to Sunday school.

Curious about origin of babies and differences between the bodies of boys and girls, men and women.

Begins to be helpful at home but forgetful of duties.

Has temper outbursts less often than before.

Less jealous of younger brothers and sisters if he has friends outside the home.

Shows less interest in relatives, more in children.

Begins to have a true understanding of right and wrong.

Is often shy with strange children, less so with strange adults.

Troublesome traits

Fights with brothers and sisters.

Bossy with younger brothers and sisters.

Fights with other children outside the home.

Tattles as a means of getting adult attention.

Exaggerates what others do or say to him.

Carries off things belonging to others.

Has temper outbursts.

Shows jealousy not only of brothers and sisters but also of other children.

Is rude and impudent, especially to people he dislikes.
Is careless about possessions and clothes.
Is noisy and thoughtless of others' property.
Insists on having his own way.
Calls people names when they cross him.
Behavior very hard to predict, moods changeable.

Special needs

Children of his own age to play with.
Plenty of space and equipment for outdoor play.
Opportunities to learn to play what other children play.
Responsibilities that are on a level with his abilities.
Opportunities to explore community under guidance.
Variety of activities.
Picture books and encouragement to look at them.

From 4 to 6   Preparation for what will be expected of him when he goes to school.
Opportunities to learn to judge time in connection with his activities.
Feeling that he is understood at home.
Plenty of affection, even if he does not show his affection for the family.

GROWTH FROM SIX TO TEN YEARS

Gradual increase in speed and accuracy in self-care activities, like bathing, dressing, and eating.
Marked resistance to going to bed at night.
Refuses to rest during the day.
Eats between meals, then dawdles over meals.
Concentrates on sweets in diet and resists milk and vegetables.
Interested in clothes but still careless of them.
Wants to dress like other children even though it may not be becoming.
Craves acceptance by those of his age.
Wants to be with playmates rather than with anyone in family.
Says he "hates" school, but goes early and stays late.
Critical of teachers and often makes fun of them.

Takes school work casually and does little study.

Upset when marks are poor but blames teacher.

Plays little with toys.

Spends most of free time playing games outdoors with classmates.

Likes to watch television whenever possible, especially at bedtime.

Uses much slang and swear words.

Talks rapidly and excitedly, often slurs words.

From 6 to 10

Has better emotional control because of pressures from his playmates to control his emotions.

Begins to worry about his school work and his abilities in sports.

Has less interest in religion, likes Sunday school mainly because he sees his friends there.

Very curious about sex matters, but talks about them mostly to his friends.

Can be very independent, but often goes back to infant ways at home to get attention or help.

Has a better understanding of right and wrong.

When he misbehaves, it is often because he believes his friends will admire him for it.

Is less interested in the family and more in outsiders.

Troublesome traits

Noisy and boisterous.

Thinks manners are "sissy stuff."

Careless about appearance and possessions.

Shirks responsibilities.

Often lies to avoid punishment or scoldings.

Insists upon doing what his friends do, and claims his parents are "mean" if they interfere.

Very afraid of what people will think of him.

Uses words of a slangy sort at embarrassing times.

Has temper outbursts at home, not outside.

From 6 to 10

Becomes overly critical of brothers and sisters, likes to argue with them, especially when parents are present.

Tells smutty jokes and stories to friends.

Likes to raid the candy box and cookie jars.

Often takes money from parents or brothers and sisters if his funds are low.

Neglects school work to play or watch television.

Special needs

From 6 to 10

Friends of his own age who are congenial and who live close enough that he can see them frequently.

Encouragement to do what he is capable of doing.

Praise for his efforts as well as his achievements.

Parental understanding that he wants friends outside and prefers their companionship to that of family.

Responsibilities that he can carry successfully.

Strict rules about daily routines to avoid carelessness.

An understanding of why he is punished when he is willfully disobedient.

The realization that he is loved in spite of his trying behavior.

Opportunities to do what his friends do.

Adequate allowance to enable him to do what his friends do.

Encouragement to stand on his own feet.

Realization that his parents are willing and able to guide him when he needs their advice.

Signs of growing up

How can a parent tell when her child is growing up?
What are the signs?

THERE are no foolproof signs of growing up. The only true indications a parent can have that her child is growing up are the changes that occur in the child's behavior. For example, take the child who has been keenly interested in playing with toys, but now begins to lose interest in toy play and uses his free time playing games with the neighborhood boys. This is a sign that he is outgrowing childish play and is moving into the stage of play that is typical of older children. In the same way, when a child loses interest in doing things with his parents and prefers to spend his time with those of his own age, we have a sign of social growing up.

In general, then, the best way to tell whether your child is moving from one stage of development to another is to watch his behavior. You cannot tell by his age alone, because the age at which children go from one stage to another varies somewhat. And it is not safe to assume that because a child is growing up in *one* phase of his development that he will automatically grow up in *all* phases. *Growth is uneven.* Sometimes a child is way ahead in some phases of his development but way behind in others.

Responsibilities

At what age should a child be given responsibilities, and how can you tell if they are right for the child?

A CHILD should be given responsibilities no later than the second year of his life. As soon as he has enough coordination to walk and to handle things without dropping them, give him simple responsibilities. These can include putting his toys on the shelves where they belong, picking up his clothes from the floor and putting them on a chair or in the laundry hamper, and carrying his empty plate or cup to the kitchen.

Each year, as he grows more mature, increase his responsibilities in difficulty and number. How rapidly and how much you can increase them will depend, of course, upon the individual child. The important thing is to get the child used to responsibilities early. Then he will not be overwhelmed when the time comes when he must assume responsibilities.

As to what responsibilities are right for a child, the only way you can tell is by the child's behavior. The child may get emotionally upset by what he is expected to do, he may do the tasks poorly and with great effort, or he may put off doing them with the excuse that he "can't do them." In that case you know the responsibilities are too great for him. But if he can handle them easily and cheerfully, you know they are suitable—and perhaps he can take a few more responsibilities without any real strain.

Troublesome children

I am the mother of three children. Dick, my youngest, has always been the most troublesome of all three. He seems to be the brightest, and I am surprised that he makes so much trouble for us at home and for his teachers at school.

DON'T be surprised because Dick causes you trouble. The brighter the child, the more troublesome he is likely to be. No, this is not because of his *brightness.* It is rather because he is advanced for his age, is capable of doing what an older child does, and yet is treated by you and his teachers like a child of his age who has only average ability. His troublesome behavior is an attempt to gain more independence. Try giving it to him, and see if he does not become less troublesome.

I think another source of trouble with your son is the fact that he is the baby of the family. The chances are that his older brothers or sisters treat him like a baby and he resents it. To let them know that he is *not* a "baby," he does many things to attract their attention, and this makes him seem like a nuisance. If they would treat him more as an equal, Dick would not cause so much trouble for them.

Slow down speed

I feel that my boy, who is just 8 years old, is too old for his age. He seems to be out of step with the things his classmates are interested in doing. How can I keep him from growing up so fast?

You can't! There is nothing you can do to control the speed of a child's development. This rate is controlled partly by his general physical condition, partly by the level of his intelligence. Certainly you would not want to injure his health in any way to retard his development—and as for his intelligence, there is nothing you can do about it. Trying to hold him back will merely result in making him unhappy. Instead, try to help him to cultivate friendships with boys whose interests and abilities are in line with your son's. Also, try to encourage him to be tolerant of the interests of his classmates so he won't feel out of step with them, or antagonize them by his "superior airs."

Changing personality

Until she was 6 years old, my daughter was a friendly, sunny-tempered, happy-go-lucky child. Now she is sensitive and touchy and seems to spend much of her time in tears. Is this a normal part of growth? How can I help her become my happy little girl again?

At six, a child often goes through this stage. Your little daughter is becoming more aware of herself as a person. She is stepping from the security of her home into the wider world of school and playmates. Her need for acceptance and approval is strong, and so she can be made unhappy by a word or look. You can help her best by being loving and understanding and by giving her a sense of warm security in her family circle. This will help her grow more sure of herself and will enable her to meet new situations happily and confidently.

chapter 3

Your child
and heredity

WHY IS your child what he is? How did he get that way? Can you predict what a child will become? Just what does a child inherit? Can training, or environment, change the traits a child is born with?

Many "old wives' tales" have been woven around these questions. But what are the *facts*?

Heredity is not a simple matter

WHAT your child is—in body and in mind—depends on what you, his parents, have made him through both the heredity and the environment you have provided him. How much he can profit by the environment you give him depends upon his inborn capacities. And these, of course, come from what he has inherited from you, his parents, and from all your ancestors.

Contrary to popular opinion, the child's heredity is *not* limited to his parents alone. No matter how remote a forefather, there is *some* contribution from that ancestor to the child born today. But, on the other hand, the contributions from his *immediate* ancestors are far more important than the influences from his more remote family.

A child's heredity comes from two long lines of ancestors, those on his mother's side of the family and those on his father's side. That is why you cannot tell before he is born what he will be like, either physically or mentally. There is an infinite number of possible combinations of traits, or tendencies, that he might inherit. You cannot tell even *after* birth what he will turn out to be! Hereditary traits are not fully developed at birth. They unfold gradually as the baby grows older.

Heredity—an intricate process

For that reason, a "wait-and-see" policy is the wisest policy to follow. Don't set your heart on having a baby with blue eyes, just because there are blue eyes on your side of the family! And don't plan your child's future career on the basis of what *you* would *like* him to be. He may inherit traits that would fit him better for a career quite different from what you had planned for him.

The importance of environment

Scientific studies of heredity have shown that a child inherits his physical and mental traits and the potentialities for some special aptitude. But will these traits and possibilities develop to their maximum? That will depend largely on the sort of environment he gets during his years of growth and development.

For example: a child with a high level of intelligence may develop into an adult with only average intellectual ability. This will happen if he has grown up in an environment that offered little opportunity for the development of his innate intelligence. Similarly, poor nutrition and lack of proper exercise, fresh air, and sunlight, will stunt the child's growth. They may even *distort* some of his physical traits, such as his teeth, the shape of his bones, and the texture of his skin.

Environment may change inherited traits

Personality—contrary to popular belief!—is not inherited. An adult's personality is the product of his training, his experiences with people, and all the factors of his environment since the moment he was born. Of course, just what *form* his personality will take will depend to some extent upon his general physical condition, his intelligence, and the special abilities (or disabilities) he has inherited.

The importance of heredity

So far we have said that heredity presents a child with certain potentialities. But heredity also *sets the limits* beyond which he cannot go. Can a person become anything he wishes to be just so long as he is willing to work long and faithfully for it? No, there is no truth in this idea. A child born with a low level of intelligence cannot hope to stand at the top of his class in school. And he won't be able to get the higher education needed to enter a profession. He will be lucky if he manages to get through elementary school.

Similarly: If he lacks the necessary ability for music or painting, *no* amount of training from the best teachers, plus any number of hours of the most careful practice, will make him more than just a very ordinary musician or painter. Nature sets a limit to which he can go. Nothing the child does will enable him to go beyond these limits.

Heredity sets the limits

Heredity or environment—which is more important? No one can say. But today the tendency is to give about equal values to both, with heredity playing a more important role in certain areas of the individual's total make-up, and environment playing the more important role in other areas.

Cooperate with nature!

Does all this sound discouraging? Perhaps, but only at first. When we give it a little more thought, we see that accepting this fact is important for everyone who is responsible for the care and guidance of a child. Knowing that a child cannot go beyond his hereditary limits enables adults to plan the guidance of the child *with the child's capacities in mind*. And, of far greater importance, it helps the adult to develop a *favorable* attitude toward the child's achievements.

This favorable attitude is of vital importance to the child's attitude *toward himself*. A child must know that he is loved, respected, and appreciated for what he has done when it is the best he is capable of doing. Only when he knows this can he have the kind of attitude toward himself that will enable him to make the most of what he has inherited.

Appreciate the child's efforts

29

Chromosomes and genes

I have heard so much about chromosomes and genes.
Just what are they?

OUR chromosomes and genes are the carriers of hereditary traits. The *chromosomes* are very tiny, string-like substances found in the sex cells of the father and mother. There are 24 of these "strings" in the male cell and 24 in the female cell. When the female cell is fertilized by the male cell, the chromosomes unite, adding up to 48 in all.

Within the chromosomes are thousands of even tinier units known as the *genes*. Each one is a carrier of a single mental or physical trait. Genes appear in more or less chance formation within the chromosomes, and are passed down from generation to generation. But in the process of cell division, before the male and female cells are ripe and ready for fertilization, some of the genes are lost. As a result, the traits in those lost genes will not be passed down to the child who will develop from the two uniting male and female cells.

It is important to realize that there is no way a person can control or determine which genes will be passed down to his child. If there is good ancestry on both sides of the family, chances are that a baby will inherit good physical and mental traits from both the mother and the father. But if there is poor ancestry on one or both sides of the family, the baby's heredity will not be of the best quality. Where this is the case, however, a good environment both before and after birth may be able to make up for some of the poor hereditary characteristics. In humans, as in animals, "good breeding" means the crossing of strains where there is good ancestry for many generations.

Some of the genes are known as *dominant,* which means that, being "stronger," they will appear in every generation. Other genes are *recessive*—they appear at varying times only, often skipping several generations. But recessive genes are always present as potentialities, and no one can predict ahead of time when they will appear. As a general rule, the recessive genes are the carriers of abnormal physical or mental traits.

Sex determination

My husband is very anxious to have a son. We now have three
daughters and I would like to have one more child.
Is there any way that I can guarantee that my child will be a boy?

IF THERE were some way to control the sex of a child, you may be sure every one would know it! The child's sex is determined by the type of sperm cell from the father that unites with the mother's ovum. There are two types of sperm cells, the X-bearing and the Y-bearing. If it is an X cell that unites with the female ovum, the child will be a girl. If it is a Y cell, the child will be a boy. But there is absolutely no way to control which of the millions of male cells released at one time will unite with the female cell and fertilize it. There are equal numbers of these two types of male cells, so there is a 50-50 chance that your next baby will be a boy.

I think it is especially important for *men* to know this scientific fact, because many men feel that it is the wife's fault that the longed-for-son is not born! The woman has *nothing* to do with the matter. It is the male cell that determines the sex of the child—and there is absolutely no way the husband can guarantee that only the Y-bearing cells from his body will come in contact with the female egg cell. The only fair attitude to take toward this matter is to be thankful that your child is strong and healthy, both physically and mentally—regardless of whether it is a girl or a boy.

Environmental influences

How important is a child's environment? What kind of environment should parents provide?

THE child's environment is of utmost importance in stimulating the growth of physical and mental traits potentially present at birth. Given a good environment, there is a good chance that these traits will develop to their fullest capacities. Without it, they will never reach their maximum potentialities.

To achieve his *physical* potentials, the child needs plenty of good food in a well balanced diet, restful sleep sufficient for his age and level of development, fresh air, sunlight, and vitamins to supplement nature's health-giving elements. And the same is true for his *mental* capacities. They can develop to their peak only if he has a good schooling which stimulates his mental abilities, combined with plenty of opportunities outside of school to broaden his cultural horizons and stimulate him to learn the things school does not teach.

No matter how great the inherited talent, it needs development and an opportunity to grow. This means special lessons in work related to that talent, and encouragement to use his top efforts to do what he is capable of. In the case of personality development, for which nature provides only the basic foundations, the child needs an environment in which he feels loved and wanted, friends who will give him fair competition, and opportunities to broaden his interests. He must learn to see himself in his true perspective. He must learn to size up his abilities and disabilities properly. From the environment provided by his parents in the home and in the neighborhood, the child will derive most of the benefits or handicaps to his physical and mental development.

Predicting sex

Can a doctor tell whether an unborn child is a boy or a girl?

Many tests have been used to predict the sex of an unborn child, but none of these has been found to be foolproof. The most widely used test to date is the heartbeat test, but this is far from certain. There are such marked variations in the rate of heartbeat of unborn children that it is impossible to tell accurately which is a boy and which a girl. Attempts have also been made to predict sex by x-rays of the bones of the unborn child. This test cannot be used until the last months of pregnancy, because of the possibility of endangering the life of the unborn child and causing sterility in the mother. Even when the test can be used safely, it, too, is not certain.

The nearest we are to a sure test for sex prediction is a study of the chemical content of the mother's saliva. This test is still in an experimental stage; so far, the results have been about 90 per cent accurate.

Not long ago a famous obstetrician said to me: "I can tell what the sex of a baby is right after birth. Before then, my guess is as good as yours, no better." Science, in other words, has not yet developed a sure test to predict the sex of an unborn child. Until it has, the wisest policy for parents to follow is to stop trying to guess what the sex of their child will be and to prepare themselves to welcome a girl as warmly and enthusiastically as a boy.

Inheritance of acquired traits

*Can a mother pass on to her child certain abilities or skills she
has learned during her lifetime? Will she, for example,
be able to transmit to her child her love for music, her ability
to write, or her skill in playing a musical instrument?*

No, only characteristics of an hereditary sort can be passed on from one generation to another. Talents of all sorts have an hereditary foundation, though the actual skills connected with them must be learned. The foundations can be, and often are, inherited by a child of a talented parent—but he must begin from the bottom and work up to the level of accomplishment achieved by his talented parent. He does not inherit the parent's level of skill.

Many children of talented parents show unusual talents similar to their parents'. Although this is due partly to their heredity, it is their environment that has also played a very important part in their achievements. These children have been brought up in a home where emphasis is put on certain activities related to the parents' talents. They have had the encouragement to develop their own innate abilities. And they have had an ever-present example to imitate in the activities of their talented parents. It is not surprising, then, that such children show abilities superior to those of children whose home environments lack activities related to these particular lines of interest and ability.

Premature birth

Is a prematurely born baby likely to develop normally or must he be carefully taken care of for the rest of his life?

IF A BABY who is born prematurely has good care, he will not only survive—he will have as good a chance of being normal or above normal in every way as a full-term baby. Some premature babies do grow into sickly, physically deformed children. But this is also true of babies who have been full term. The percentages are about the same for both types.

As for mental abilities, prematurity does *not* affect intelligence. There are, of course, some feebleminded children among those born before term, but the percentage of such cases is not higher than for those not premature. There is evidence, however, that prematurely born children are more nervous and high strung, have more personality disturbances, and are more often "problem children" than is true for those who were not premature.

But this is not because the children were premature. Rather, it is because of the overprotective, oversolicitous attitude of the *parents*. Parents are likely to feel that because a child was small and delicate at birth, due to being born too soon, he will always be so. As a result, they treat him as if he were a weakling, and in many cases make him a badly adjusted individual.

Twins

I have twins, a boy and a girl. They are very different in every way. I thought twins were supposed to be alike.

THERE are two types of twins, *identical* and *non-identical*. Identical twins are so much alike that it is often difficult to tell which is which. Mentally and temperamentally they are alike, too. The reason for this similarity is that they have both come from the same fertilized egg which split into two distinct parts in the early stages of cell division. As a result, the two children have the same hereditary carriers—chromosomes and genes—and they are always of the same sex.

Your two children cannot be identical because they are not of the same sex. This type of twins, the non-identical, comes from two egg cells from the mother that have been fertilized at the same time by two separate and distinct cells from the father. Because each fertilized egg has its own chromosomes and genes, it is likely that the two children will be no more alike than ordinary brothers and sisters who are born at different times.

33

It is true that your twins shared the same prenatal environment. And doubtless you have brought them up together so that they have shared much the same environment ever since they were born. Nevertheless, they are different because of the differences in their hereditary endowments. So don't try to force them into the same pattern any more than you would if they were not twins. Let each develop his own personality and his own individuality. Only if you do this can you hope to have happy, well-adjusted children.

Inheritance of personality difficulties

My 8-year-old son is so much like his father in appearance and personality that everyone remarks on it. But there is one thing that troubles me. My husband rarely loses his temper, but when he does become angry, he will go into a complete silence and sulk for a week. Now my son is beginning to have sulky periods. Is this inherited from his father? How can I help my boy overcome this habit?

THE TENDENCY to sulkiness may be inherited, but it is also partly a result of your husband's actions. Your son is unconsciously copying his father. To help him overcome this behavior pattern, try to stop his sulky actions the moment they begin. At the first sign, send him to his room and tell him he can come out the minute he can smile again. If you do this pleasantly, firmly, and consistently, he will soon learn that he gains nothing by sulking and will stop.

The baby's place
in your family

MONTHS before your baby arrives you will be preparing a
place for him in your home. As small and crowded as your home
may be, somehow you will manage to make space for this newest
member of the family. But in the same way, you must prepare
the family to make a place in their hearts and in their lives for
this newcomer. This is an emotional or psychological preparation—far more important than the physical preparation of baby
clothes or a nursery.

Getting ready for the baby

DOES THE FAMILY look forward to the new baby's arrival
with feelings of doubt and worry? with regret? or with eager
welcome? The family's feelings are important, because they
will determine, largely, how the family greets the baby when
he finally does come into the house. And responsibility for this
readiness is mainly the *mother's*.

Perhaps the father-to-be is anxious to have a baby, but

35

wonders—if it is the first baby—what about the safety of child-birth, his wife's health, and will her attitude towards him change as she takes on the job of motherhood? Will the baby's coming make serious changes in the established pattern of his life? What financial problems will the baby bring? If there are already children in the home, the father's worry about finances may be very real, and may overcloud the joy of anticipation he would otherwise experience.

Mother has the main job

Where the family already has one or more children, what place the new baby will have depends largely on the mother. If she is so completely taken up with the care of the new baby that she neglects the other children, they will naturally resent the "intruder" and refuse to accept him. But if she shares her pleasures and attentions with the other children, they will welcome the newcomer into their home and their hearts. From the beginning they will make him feel that he, too, is an important member of the family.

Helping him find a place

As THE BABY becomes a toddler and grows into childhood, his place in the family should become more and more clearly defined. He needs to have set aside for him a place of his own, for *his* clothes, *his* toys, *his* books, *his* pets. And every one must recognize that only *he* owns this area and respect it to the point where no one will intrude without first asking permission. His toys and his clothes should be *his*—with no borrowing without his permission first.

Preparing baby's brothers and sisters

Of course he will seem babyish to his older brothers and sisters, but this should not give them the right to push him around and announce that he is a nuisance. Mother and father must encourage the other children to be tolerant and under-standing of his level of development. The youngest must be given a chance to feel loved and wanted in the home. If he is allowed to feel that he is rejected by his brothers and sisters, the whole pattern of his personality may be distorted.

He is bound to be different from the older children in the family. After all, he is not only younger and less developed, but he also has a different hereditary background. That is why he is the very special individual that he is. Every member of the family, from the youngest child to the oldest grandparent, must recognize and accept this. They must love and admire him for what he is—no matter how different his abilities and his interests. Only when they do this can the baby feel that he has a real place in the home, and that he is a real and important member of the family group.

Oldest child

Our oldest child resents taking care of the baby. I have three other children and I feel that Marie, who is 10 years old, is old enough to help with the baby and with the housework. She seems to feel that she is being "picked on."

Have you made the care of the baby a *treat* rather than a duty for your daughter? Surely she must like to do things for the baby and this will free you for the household jobs. Have your three other children do routine jobs in the home and thus take some of the burden off your shoulders and Marie's. You do not want your baby to grow up with the feeling that he is a nuisance to the family and that his presence in the home means overwork for you or Marie. If the whole family can share the care of the baby with you and Marie, and thus give him contacts with the entire family, he will grow up with a feeling of being just as much a part of the family as the other members.

Family upsets

Should a baby upset the entire family's life? We have a new baby and I find that my wife is so busy with the care of the baby that the two other children and I get somewhat pushed aside. How much attention should a baby receive?

A baby should receive enough attention to see that his physical needs are taken care of and that a reasonable portion of his waking time is spent in contact with people. A mother who has had two children should not find the care of a baby very difficult. Surely your wife knows the routine of baby care by now. While she is doing things for the baby, such as bathing or feeding him, she can talk to the two older children. When she takes the baby outside for an airing in his carriage, the other children can come along. And, when the baby is sleeping, she can do things for them and have them with her.

If you and the older children lend a hand with the housework and the care of the baby, it will give your wife more time to be with you and the children. Taking care of two children, a baby, and a household is a full-time job for any woman. You cannot expect your wife to have much time to do things for or with you unless

.you help her with the work. Also, you must expect the family routine to be upset temporarily until the new baby can be fitted into the family schedule. This is only for a short time, so do not allow it to disturb you.

Age differences

We have two teen-age children, a son and a daughter. I am having a new baby soon and I am afraid the children will make the baby feel very unwelcome as they are both upset about my having the baby. I do not want the baby to feel that he has no place in the family or that he is unwanted.

OF COURSE you do not want your baby to feel unwanted and unloved. At the same time, it is quite understandable that your teen-age children look forward to the baby's arrival with annoyance. After all, the baby will disrupt the pattern of their lives, and make a lot of noise and confusion in the home.

But there are some things you can do about this situation. Try to plan, before your baby's arrival, a schedule of duties that will not interfere too much with the established pattern of the home. Put the baby in a room as remote from the older children as possible so the baby's crying will not disturb their sleep, studies, or entertainment of their friends. And do not economize on their clothes or spending money unless absolutely necessary.

Once the baby has arrived, I am sure they will be as excited about it as you are. Let them play with the baby and help you with its care from time to time, but never insist that they baby-sit at a time they have things they want to do with their friends. And when the baby becomes a troublesome toddler, keep him under control so that your older children's prized possessions are not torn to pieces or broken.

chapter 5

What about schedules?

O<small>F COURSE</small> a baby needs a schedule, just as you and I do. People can't live harmoniously in today's world without *some* pattern to their daily lives. Besides, to function efficiently our body needs to be trained to perform in a set, routine manner. But this just doesn't happen without good training in the early years.

We know that no two babies are alike, and that no two families live alike. That's why we can't set up *one* schedule that will fit all babies. No, a baby's schedule must be tailor-made. It must be planned to meet *his* needs, his age, his general health. But we also have to consider the needs and demands of the rest of the family.

A ready-made schedule won't fit all babies

Schedules on demand

F<small>OR</small> the first two or three months of his life, it's impossible to keep a baby on a rigid schedule. Because his nervous system is not yet mature, the baby can't function in a fixed, rigid manner. He doesn't get hungry always at the same time. He can't always take the same quantity of food. And on Tuesday he doesn't need the same amount of sleep that he needed on Monday.

Today's doctors are becoming more and more aware of this fact. That is why they are not prescribing the same rigid schedules they did a few years ago. They are urging parents to be more flexible in following schedules. There is even a trend to urge parents to let the baby *set his own schedule*, according to his own needs and demands.

A flexible schedule is desirable

This is certainly the wisest approach because it does consider the *individual* needs of the baby. This way we don't try to force the baby into a pattern that fitted an older brother or sister, or the neighbor's baby. Instead, we put the baby on a schedule made to order *for him.*

By the end of his second month—or certainly a month later—your baby's behavior will give you a clue as to what his schedule will be. He will waken at predictable times and cry, letting you know he's hungry. He will urinate and move his bowels at much the same time day after day. And, at much the same times of the day or night, he will yawn, look sleepy, and show little interest in what goes on around him.

What to look for

Watch for these signs. They mean that the baby is setting his own schedule and is ready to keep to it. Of course, you may have to adjust the schedule to fit it into the family routine. But the more closely you can keep to the schedule that fits your baby's needs, the more quickly will the pattern of his life fall into a regular routine. Make major changes only when your doctor feels they should be made.

Timing is important

Dᴜʀɪɴɢ the first two years of his life—until the habits of eating, sleeping, and eliminating are well established—it is very important to keep your baby on a strict schedule. But don't prolong this without end. As the child grows older, he will need to adapt himself to emergencies from time to time. This will be difficult and upsetting for a child whose schedule has always been rigid. For that reason, it's a good idea to introduce slight changes in schedule when the baby is 3 or 4 years old.

Your timing of these changes is very important. For example, it is never wise to keep a young child up beyond his usual bedtime when his behavior shows that he is sleepy and tired. But suppose he has had a good nap, is full of energy and in good spirits. *That* is the time to introduce a variation from the usual bedtime routine. Let him stay up a trifle longer than usual, but not long enough to become tired and fretful.

A parent's *attitude* toward the baby's schedule is of greatest importance. If a parent is lax about schedules and does things for a baby to suit adult convenience, the baby suffers from lack of routine in his life. There's another side to the picture, of course. Sticking to schedules too strictly is likely to mean tension in the parent. In her desire to get her baby into bed on the dot, or to have his meal ready at the exact scheduled time, the mother becomes nervous and tense. And this condition interferes with the forming of good sleep or eating habits. In other words, the formation of good habits requires a *reasonably* strict following of schedule *together* with a relaxed, calm manner in the mother.

Use judgment when you vary baby's routine

Self-demand feeding

Just what is "self-demand feeding"? Is it approved by doctors today?

"SELF-DEMAND feeding" means feeding a baby when he cries and thus shows that he is hungry. It is based on the idea that the baby, by crying, will let you know when he is hungry.

Today, doctors prefer varying the feeding time to meet the baby's needs instead of trying to put a young baby on a rigid schedule. No, this is not a *new* theory; it has been used for generations. Today we realize that we can't expect young babies to be hungry at exactly the same time day after day. That is why many doctors are recommending that the feeding schedule be fixed by the baby's demands, as expressed in his cries—and not by the clock.

Baby's bath

When is the best time to bathe a baby?

THERE is no "best time." The bath schedule should be set partly to suit the mother's convenience, and partly to fit the baby's eating and sleeping schedule. When a mother has only one baby to take care of, perhaps the best time for the bath is in the middle of the morning, after the housework is done. This leaves the afternoon free for going out when the weather is good. If there is another child who is too young to be in school, the mother may prefer to bathe the baby while the older child is napping.

No matter when the bath is given, it is wise to follow it by feeding and a nap. Never bathe the baby just before taking him out for his airing—he may catch cold. And it isn't a good idea to bathe him in the evening—he's likely to be fussy and object to being bathed when he would rather sleep.

Interrupting schedules

Many times, over weekends or on holidays, relatives or friends drop in just as I am about to feed the children or put them to bed. Should I interrupt their schedules and allow them to be with the company?

Young children resent being pushed aside when there is company. They like to be in the midst of what is going on. Give them an opportunity to be with your guest for a few minutes, then excuse yourself and continue with the scheduled activities. If a guest is fond of children, he or she might like to take over feeding the children or helping put them to bed. A bedtime story from a guest, or someone to sit with them while they are eating supper, usually eliminates any fussing at having to go to bed when company is around.

Not until children are 5 or 6 years old should you interrupt their schedules too sharply. Hungry or tired children become fretful. They put on scenes that are embarrassing for the parents and unpleasant for the guests.

Free time

When my children have any free time, after breakfast or while I am preparing supper, they always ask me what they can do. Should I schedule all of their time so they'll have something to do every minute they're awake?

A child needs time to relax, to free himself from tensions, to do much as he pleases. There is nothing worse for a child than to have every minute of his waking life planned and organized. When your children ask you what they can do, put the responsibility right back on *their* shoulders. Ask them, "What would you like to do?" Every child must learn to take the initiative in planning his own activities.

That is why it is wise, even during the first year of life, to schedule the baby's time so that he has some *free* time every day. Give him toys and let *him* take the lead in what he will do. Remember: you can't tell your child what to do *all* his life! *Now* is the time for him to learn to be independent in planning the use of his time.

Resentment against schedules

My husband says that the strict schedule the doctor has advised for our 6-month-old baby is "all nonsense." He claims the baby should be able to adjust to changes in his routine, especially when my husband wants to sleep late or stay at friends' homes until after the baby's bedtime. Is he right about this?

IN a year or two, yes, your husband will be right in what he says about the baby's adjusting to changes in his schedule, but right now, *no*. A baby as young as yours needs a definite routine—especially as your doctor has ordered it.

Try to show your husband the need for this. Urge him to make the necessary sacrifices in his own pleasures for the sake of your baby's health. Point out to him also that when a young baby's schedule is seriously and frequently disrupted, the baby becomes fretful. Under such conditions, how could your husband enjoy the pleasures you mention?

Different schedules

How can a mother manage when she has three children, all on different schedules?

DURING a child's early years, he must have a schedule suited to his needs and his level of development. This, I know, makes a heavy burden for the mother. But, as children reach the second or certainly the third year, their schedules can be much the same except that the older child will stay up later than the younger, and take a shorter nap or rest period in the afternoon.

Work out a plan for taking care of your three children so you can do things for one child while another is sleeping, playing, or eating. I know this takes much skill, and it will keep you stepping most of the day—but it lasts for only a few years.

If you find your children's schedules do not dovetail very satisfactorily, then adjust the older children's schedules to fit into the baby's schedule. A baby must be kept on a stricter schedule than a toddler or a school child. To a certain extent, the family routine must be fitted into the baby's schedule.

43

chapter 6

The why of crying

Uᴺᴛɪʟ a baby can use gestures, *crying* is his only way of telling us something. But we forget that, sometimes. Many people think the baby is crying just to annoy you, or to make you pay attention. When he is six months to a year old, this *may* be the baby's reason for crying. *Before* that time, his cries are appeals for help. He is trying to tell you that something is the matter with him and that he needs you.

The baby's first cries all sound much the same. Of course, some are louder and stronger than others. When a baby is tired, his cries are weak; when he is rested, they are loud and piercing. But the *tone* quality of all his cries is about the same. Therefore, his cries are not much help in letting you know what's wrong with him or what he wants. All they tell you is that he is in some sort of trouble and needs you.

Finding out what is wrong

About all you can do, then, is to try one thing after another until you find the cause of the trouble. Is he hungry? Is he suffering gas pains and in need of burping? Is he uncomfortable from lying in the same position for too long? Or is he in actual pain? When you have found the cause of his crying, he will stop.

44

B<small>Y THE</small> time a baby is 3 or 4 months old, you begin to hear differences in the strength as well as in the quality of tone of his cries. His cries tell you more than they did at first. Listen closely to the cries of a 5 or 6 month old baby, and you can tell pretty accurately what is the matter with him and what he wants.

A *hunger* cry and a *pain* cry are both usually loud and piercing. However, the hungry baby interrupts *his* cries to make sucking movements with his lips, while the baby who is in pain cries harder and longer with no time out even for a breath. The *sleepy* cry is a kind of moaning, together with yawns.

Spoiled crying, or crying to win attention, generally appears around the sixth month. By that time, the baby is aware of the people around him. He wants to have someone talk to him, pick him up, play with him. If he doesn't get the attention he wants, he protests. As soon as someone comes to see what is the matter, his cries disappear as if by magic, and his face is wreathed in smiles. You don't have to be a mind reader to know that the only thing that was the matter with *him* was that he wanted attention!

Hunger, pain and sleepiness

Crying for attention

C<small>RYING</small> is exhausting for a baby, for he really cries with his whole body. His nervous system is not yet mature, so he uses up energy in two ways: through his cries, and through the kicking of his legs, waving of his arms, and twisting of his entire body while he is crying. After a long cry, the baby is so worn out he drops off to sleep because he has no energy left to cry any more. Babies can't afford to use up their supply of energy for crying. They need *all* their strength and energy for the process of growing into normal, healthy individuals.

At all times, a baby's cries should be heeded. There are two reasons why this is essential. *First,* that's how to find out what is the matter with him. *Second,* the baby develops a sense of security when he knows there is someone available to take care of him when he needs care. Although they don't have definite proof, experts believe they know the origin of many twisted personalities. They blame the feelings of insecurity

Two reasons for answering cries

45

and frustration that often develop in the early months of life when a baby's cries are ignored.

Go to the baby when he cries. From the way he responds, you can quickly discover whether his cry was a call for help or a bid for attention. If all he wanted was attention, he will stop crying and show delight that he was able to get what he wanted. But if he really needed your help, he will still cry, even though you are with him. In fact, his crying will increase until you find and correct the cause of the trouble.

Substitutes for crying

B Y THEIR second birthday, most babies can say a few words. Week by week their stock of words increases. They learn to put words together into sentences. There is less need for crying as the toddler learns that he can make more headway by *asking* for what he wants. The sooner he learns this, the better, because once crying becomes set into a habit pattern, it is hard to get rid of.

Handling crying in toddlers

You *can* do something about the child who is half-way between babyish crying and more mature speech. Insist that he *ask* for what he wants. Refuse it when he cries for it. This may mean a few embarrassing experiences for parents, but it is well worth it for the child's sake.

The days of crying girls are over. Today, we expect girls— just like boys—to put crying away with their baby clothes. Any child who persists in crying long after the time when it is necessary is soon nicknamed "Crybaby," a name that shows friends' contempt for such babyish ways. Only when there is a real hurt will the child's friends accept the crying. That is why it is so important for parents to help their child substitute *speech* for crying as early as possible. It should be done before the crying habit has taken root.

"Tell me what you want"

We should remember that young children often do not realize that there are other ways of getting what they want besides crying. It is up to the parents to teach them this. The way to do it is not by scolding a child or by trying to shame him out of his crying ways. We need a more constructive approach. Tell the child you don't know what he wants when he cries, and ask him to *tell* you. Refuse to give him what he is crying for until he stops and puts his wishes into words. Most children learn very quickly when handled in this way.

Crying it out

*My baby is 5 months old. When he cries friends advise
me to let him cry it out. They say I'll spoil
him if I go to him every time he cries. Is that right?*

No, NOT for a baby his age (yes, if he were 6 or 8 months older). *Your* baby
is too young to be crying just to get attention. He wants help, so you should see
what is the matter. If you let him cry it out, he will cry until he's worn out and
drop off to sleep. As I have already pointed out, this is bad for two reasons. First:
lengthy crying is too exhausting for baby; he needs his strength for *growing*, not
crying. Second: your refusal to go to him when he cries gives him a feeling of
fright and insecurity. This may do permanent harm to his personality.

Stopping crying

*When my baby starts to cry, she becomes almost hysterical.
I then find it very hard to stop her crying unless
I pick her up, rock her, or play with her. I am afraid
this will spoil her. What do you think?*

YES, your baby will get so used to the attention she wins after a crying attack
that she will not be satisfied unless she keeps getting it. Try to get to your baby
sooner when she starts to cry, *before* she can work herself up into an hysterical fit.

It is only when crying is prolonged without any attention that it becomes
hysterical. It isn't likely in the early stages. That is a good reason for you to plan
to do things near your baby's room at those times of day when she most often
starts her crying. Then you can go to her quickly, and in that way forestall the
hysteria.

Home "crybaby"

*My 8-year-old Harold is a terrible crybaby at home. He is very
popular with the boys and I am sure he would not be
if he cried around them. His teacher says he never cries in
school. How can I stop his crying at home?*

HAROLD is quite old enough to listen to reason. Just tell him that crying is
babyish and that if he persists in crying at home, sooner or later this habit will
make him cry at school or when he is with the boys. This will make him stop
and think twice before crying at home. If he does keep it up, remind him of how

habits work. Explain how habits will show up anywhere. And don't give him what he wants when he cries. Sympathize with him only when you know he has been badly hurt or is in real pain.

Tears

When my son, age 4, cries, he screams and kicks, but I see no sign of tears. Is this crying or temper?

CRYING doesn't always bring tears to the eyes. Kicks and screams in a 4-year-old are not part of crying, either. I would call your son's behavior a temper tantrum.

Handle this the same as you would crying. Explain to him he will not get what he wants when he screams for it, and that you will pay no attention whatever to him. The next time he puts on this scene, walk out of the room, shut the door, and pay no attention to him. It may take a few experiences like this to convince him that you mean what you say. Even if it is nerve-racking for you, it will be worth it!

Embarrassing scenes

My 5-year-old is a genius in using tears at a time when he knows that he will embarrass us. The result is we're well under his thumb! He seldom cries at home, but when we are on the street, in a bus, or with friends, he starts to cry when we say "No!"

IF your son is smart enough to have learned that crying will not get him what he wants at home, then he is smart enough to learn crying will not help him outside the home either. But so far, he has not had to learn this. That is *your* fault, not his.

You can start at once to mend your ways. Tell your child right now that the next time he cries in public, you will pay no attention to him, that you will even try to pretend he is not your son. Tell him you don't want people to think *your* son is a crybaby. *Then live up to your word.* No matter how embarrassing the experience may be for you, stick it out. It should take only a few such experiences for your son to learn that you meant what you said.

chapter 7

Bed –
or bedlam?

$\mathbf{M}$OST little children go to bed willingly—until they reach their second birthday. It's at two that almost always they seem to get the idea they are too old to need sleep. They think it is more fun to stay up so they can see what is going on in the home.

At this age, the child is not mature enough to realize that he is tired or sleepy. He can't see that his fussiness is a sign of fatigue and sleepiness. He thinks only of the good times the family is having—and resents the thought of what *he* will miss if he goes to bed.

Two methods of attack

$\mathbf{H}$OW DO *you* treat this early sign that your child is asserting his independence? When bedtime comes, is your home a madhouse, or does your child accept bedtime as a part of the day's routine, the same as meals and play? What *you* do about it is important because, for many years to come, it will mean the difference between bed and bedlam.

If *you* make an issue of your child's going to bed, *he* will, too. After all, the only model a little child can copy is his parents. If it is all right for *you* to make a fuss and get angry when it is time for him to go to bed, why isn't it all right for him, too? It is natural for the young child to reason this way. You have to be prepared to meet this reasoning in a manner that will not pave the way for years of trouble ahead.

The wrong method

But suppose you approach the bedtime problem in a matter-of-fact manner. Suppose you make it a *pleasant* experience, so that the child's last hour before bedtime is pleasant for him. Then he learns to go off to bed in a cheerful, matter-of-fact manner. He welcomes the pleasant end to a pleasant day.

A 2-year-old is a balky, contrary creature. "No!" seems to be the main word in his vocabulary. He delights in doing just the opposite of what you ask him to do. That is why parents need tremendous tact and understanding to prevent the opposition, the battle of wits between parents and child, that just seems to make a bad situation worse. Recognizing that a child of this age will try to have his own way at any cost is very important. It will put you on your guard and make you use different tactics than if he were older and able to understand the value of enough sleep.

Try to fore-stall the NO's

Handling bedtime resistance

CHILDREN resist not only going to bed at night, but daily naps, too. Mother, of course, knows that a child who is full of energy and has enjoyed a morning of vigorous play, needs his rest in the middle of the day. Otherwise he will become so tired and fretful that, when night comes, he will be overtired and unable to sleep. And the night bed hour will mean chaos for the whole family.

The problem of naps

Knowing this, the mother is often overly concerned and insistent that the child have a nap. The more she insists, the more the child resists. The result? Naptime is bedlam—with the mother losing her temper, the child losing *his,* and no one getting any rest or relaxation.

You're probably thinking, "No child can realize that he needs his rest. And you can't argue with him and explain facts as you can with an older child." That is true. At the same time, though he must have his rest, he cannot get it if he goes to bed with a resisting attitude. Such an attitude makes relaxation impossible—and relaxation is a necessary part of sleepiness. Clearly, it is better to send him off to bed *willingly*. But how can this attitude of willingness be achieved? How *can* parents deal with this problem of bedtime resistance?

First—and foremost—don't let bed be linked with unpleasantness. Never send your child to bed as a form of punishment—not even if you know his naughtiness stems from the fact that he is overtired. Treat the naughty act first. Then, when that situation is cleared up, send him to bed. In this way, he will not associate going to bed with punishment. He will not build up a resisting attitude toward going to bed.

Bed should never mean punishment

Bedtime can be pleasant

Make going to bed a pleasant experience for your child, so that he will go willingly. Here are three ways to do this:

1. *Allow plenty of time for preparation for bed.* That helps to make it a pleasant and leisurely experience. Even if some unexpected thing happens so that the child is running behind schedule, don't penalize him by trying to hurry him. This will only excite him and interfere with the relaxed attitude that is so essential to sleep. Hurrying him will also very likely lead him to resist. It is far better to get him to bed a few minutes late than to get him in bed on time, but in a mood that will make sleep impossible.

Bedtime should not be hurried

2. *Establish a bedtime ritual that will be carried out every night.* First get the child ready for bed. Then let him put his toys to bed, and his pet, if he has one. Next, time for his own bedtime play with you. Read him stories, show him pictures, play some tunes on a nursery phonograph, or sing to him. Choose what appeals to him and relaxes him. Then, after he has said his prayers, cover him up and turn off the lights.

At first you may feel that a ritual like this is too time-consuming for a busy mother to undertake. But it's worth the time it takes, even if it means leaving the dinner dishes in the sink to be washed later. In the end, it is no more time-consuming than quieting a child who has been rushed to bed and who protests staying there. Besides, when there are several children in the family, one of the older children, or perhaps

The dishes can usually wait

51

the father, may be able to take over the responsibility for this routine.

3. *Be sure to ask your child if he is completely ready for bed before the lights are turned off.* Go over the usual list of things a child wants after he is in bed: going to the toilet, a drink of water, his favorite toy, or some other excuse he will think of to get out of bed. If he has told you that he wants nothing, he will be far less likely to call you back than if you had not checked with him before leaving him. Follow the same policy at nap time to forestall possible trouble.

Bath time

I find it quite a rush to get the children bathed before supper. They are 2 and 4 years old and play very vigorously. As a result, they are dirty when they come in. Is it better to give the baths after their supper?

A BATH is always a relaxing experience for children, especially when they are tired. You will find that they will eat their suppers better, and will be more relaxed and ready to go to sleep at bedtime, if they have their baths *after* their hard play. Of course, this will mean a rush for *you,* but you could make the preliminary preparations for their supper *before* they come in from play. You can probably manage their baths before supper time if you bring them in from play a half hour earlier, or else delay their supper a bit.

Resentment of older children

My 3-year-old Richard puts up a fuss every day at nap time and again at bedtime. He claims he isn't being treated fairly, as his older brothers and sisters don't have to take naps and they can stay up later than he. How can I argue against this and convince him?

IT IS hard to argue with a 3-year-old, and even harder to convince him, that your restrictions on his behavior are fair. He doesn't understand why *he* cannot do what the older children do. Perhaps the most effective approach to your problem is this: Keep pointing out to Richard that next year he will be able to stay up until a certain time; a year later, a little longer; and so on. Also, explain that when he goes to school he will no longer need a nap or rest in the afternoon. But make these promises with the understanding that he follows with reasonable willingness the times you set for his bedtime *now.*

52

Baby sitter

When we go out evenings, I have a high school girl
as a baby sitter. She is lax, lets them get up and run around,
call for a drink of water, or to go to the toilet.
They don't get enough sleep and are tired and fretful the next day.
Baby sitters are hard to get so I hesitate to let her go.

You cannot expect a young high school girl who comes into your home only once in a while to keep the same order and discipline that you or a more experienced person can. I suggest you ask the minister of your church if he knows of an older woman of the congregation who would be available as a sitter. You and your husband should be able to have occasional evenings off for the pleasures you enjoy. At the same time, you should not have to pay the penalty the next day by having your children cross and unruly. An older person makes a better baby sitter than a high school girl because of longer experience. Also, children are more likely to conform to family rules when an older person is in charge than when the sitter is only slightly older than they themselves.

Bedtime games

After supper, my husband likes to play with our children, who are 2, 4, and
6 years of age. I notice this excites the children and it is then hard
to get them to bed and to sleep. My husband gets home just before the
baby goes to bed, and this is his only time to play with the children.
Should I deprive him and the children of this play time?

No, do not put an end to the play time your husband and children have together. And yet, it isn't fair to your children to have them so excited at bedtime that they cannot fall asleep. Could you not persuade your husband to use his time with the children in stories and other amusements that will not excite them? In this way, he could have time to be with the children and to get to know them, without injurious results. Weekends and holidays, when your husband is at home all day, it should be less of a problem. They can play exciting games at times of the day when this will not interfere with the children's sleep.

Bedtime stories

What types of stories are best to tell or read to children at bedtime?

At bedtime, avoid all stories that are exciting because of their action. Also, avoid stories that arouse a child's curiosity and start him guessing. Fairy tales and all stories with a mystery element are examples. Stories safe for bedtime are those about nature and about familiar people doing familiar things. Poetry is especially good for bedtime reading, because the rhythm has a soothing effect on the child and relaxes him while he should be getting ready to sleep.

Bedtime fears

My daughter is ten years old. She is a fearless, self-reliant child and has never had a night light in her bedroom or seemed to want one. Now, suddenly, she begs me to leave the light on when she goes to bed and says she is afraid to go to sleep in the dark. My husband thinks we should let her have her way, but I do not want to encourage her to give in to her fear. Do you think I should let her have a light on at night?

CHILDREN often go through a period when they are afraid of the dark. Sometimes a tree tapping at a window or a shadow cast by a curtain can frighten them. Since your daughter is usually a fearless child, I would let her have her way. If you do not approve of a night light in her bedroom, you might let her keep her door open at night so light from the hall can shine in. She will probably outgrow this fear of darkness quickly if little fuss is made over it.

Prayers

Ever since my children have been old enough to do so, they have said the children's prayer, "Now I lay me down to sleep." Recently, my older child, who is 6, has been asking questions about the possibility of dying during the night. I think this idea has come from the prayer. Can you suggest another prayer I could substitute for it?

WHY not discuss this problem with your clergyman? Ask him to recommend another prayer for your children, one that will not refer to dying during the night. There are many prayers, just as suitable for children, that do not raise doubt in their minds about the chances of living through the night. You will find a carefully chosen selection of these in the Prayers and Graces section of *The Bible Story Hour*, Standard Educational Corporation.

chapter 8

Thumb
sucking

W<small>HAT</small> sort of satisfaction does the thumb-sucker get? For sucking his thumb does give him satisfaction, no one can deny. And why can't he get just as much pleasure in some other way?

The fact is that he *could* get satisfaction in some other way—*if only he knew where to turn!* This is where his parents and teachers have a duty. *They* are the ones who, because of their experience and knowledge, can show him where to turn for satisfaction whenever he is tempted to suck his thumb.

Whys of thumb sucking

W<small>HY</small> do babies suck their thumbs? And why do children continue to do it long after they have graduated from nipple or bottle? Scientific studies of babies agree on these two points: *First,* the child gets satisfaction from sucking. *Second,* in the absence of a nipple or bottle, he will turn to the next best thing within reach—his thumb.

Scientists have also explained why some babies suck

their thumbs more than others, and why some persist in sucking as late as the college age. Experts blame faulty feeding habits in babyhood. They point to the too rigid feeding schedule that expects the baby to get hungry only when the clock says it is time to eat, *not* when the hunger pangs of his stomach tell him it is time for the breast or bottle. A hungry baby will suck on anything he can get into his mouth because this relieves some of the pain that hunger brings. When he can't get the breast or bottle, at least he can turn to his thumb.

A cause: bad feeding habits in babyhood

Not enough time for sucking and not enough food to satisfy the baby's needs—these are also faulty feeding habits. Sometimes the baby is limited by a rigid feeding schedule to just so many minutes for his meal. Often he is not satisfied when his source of food is abruptly taken from him. Perhaps he sucks vigorously in the time given him—but there just isn't enough food for him. Perhaps he can not get it quickly enough, because of the small holes in the bottle. Or perhaps the holes are *too* big, so that he gets all the food he can hold with too little sucking. This, too, leads to feelings of frustration which the baby may express by sucking his thumb after the nipple has been taken away.

Check on baby's feeding schedule

Some other reasons

W HEN babies are weaned from breast or bottle, and are fed with a spoon, they often miss the familiar, pleasant sensation of sucking. When this happens, it means that a baby is not yet ready for this more mature form of feeding. It is better to make the change-over more slowly, giving him some opportunity for sucking. At the same time, gradually get him used to taking his food from a spoon.

Change should be gradual

As the baby becomes a toddler, and then a pre-schooler or even a school child, he may, through habit, turn back to infantile forms of satisfaction. This is likely when he is tired, nervous, or out of sorts because things have not been going to his liking. Several things may make him unhappy, and lead him to seek satisfaction from the old, familiar experience of sucking. One may be the new baby in the family who is occupying the mother's time and attention, and pushing *him* into the background. Another may be the unpleasant experience he meets when out in the yard playing with other children. So his thumb goes into his mouth and he sucks.

Unhappiness may reawaken an old habit

All babies do some thumb sucking, at least until they are 9 months to a year old. Only when the baby is an *excessive* sucker, or when the sucking persists month after month, with no visible sign of lessening, is it time for parents to be concerned. Try to figure out *why* the baby sticks to a habit he should have pushed into the background with other forms of infantile behavior. If you can't find why, the best thing to do is to get a doctor's advice.

Will thumb sucking just vanish of its own accord? It may or it may not. Suppose it persists long beyond the usual age. Then it is a safe guess that it is developing into a habit that, like all habits, will last until some substitute source of satisfaction can replace it. It will be up to you, the parent, to find out what will take the place of the satisfaction your baby has been getting from sucking his thumb. This may take time. It will certainly take skill.

When to take action

Five suggestions

Here are some suggestions to help you solve this problem:

1. Each day, give your baby some chance to suck milk or juice from a bottle. Even if this has been taken from him, give it back. Perhaps you took it away too soon, or too abruptly. Let *him* decide when he wants to give up the bottle.

2. Examine *your own* behavior and your attitude toward your child. Are you doing something that is giving him the feeling that you no longer love him as you did before? Do you have less time for him than you used to? Is your interest in him less than when he was younger? If so, mend your ways. No matter that your day is filled to overflowing with the care of younger children! Save some time for *him* so that he can feel secure in your interest and love.

Perhaps you are at fault

3. Go over your child's daily schedule. Is it too rigid for his age? Does it make him nervous? Does he show by his behavior that he is pressed to the point where he is nervous, irritable, and given to temper outbursts? If "Yes" is the answer, let up a bit here and there, so your child can do things at *his* own pace, not yours.

A change in schedule may help

4. Keep a record of the times when your child does most of his thumb sucking. Do they come when he is tired, sleepy, hungry, or nervous? Or do they follow punishments, scoldings, or signs of your own irritation? Chances are that this record

will give you a real clue as to what is back of the thumb sucking.

Help those hands keep busy

5. Little hands are ready for action most of the time. Does your child have enough to keep his hands busy? You can't expect him to take over adult duties or responsibilities, but you *can* give him something to do with his hands. When his hands are idle and you see the thumb moving to his mouth, think of it as a signal that he wants something to do with his hands. Why not give him a favorite toy to play with, or invite him to join you in what you are doing? Hands that are busy are not likely to find their way to a child's mouth.

Mechanical restraints

My 18-month-old son is a thumb-sucker. My mother has advised me to put a little metal cage on his thumb so he won't suck. One of my friends uses splints on her child's arms so he can't bend his elbows. Do these really work?

ANY KIND of mechanical restraint will "work" as long as the restraints are used. But just as soon as you remove them, right back into the mouth goes the thumb. These restraints do not get at the *root* of the trouble and, therefore, are not a real cure. Besides, they are very likely to increase nervous tension and lead to a resentful attitude in the child. This *increases* the amount of thumb sucking as soon as the restraints are taken away. Instead of trying to prevent thumb sucking mechanically, you would do better to try to find the *cause* of the sucking and then correct the cause.

Crooked teeth

Is it true that crooked or protruding teeth come from thumb sucking?

DOCTORS do not all agree as to how much thumb sucking affects the shape of the child's jaw. But most of them do agree that before the baby has any teeth, thumb sucking has no effect at all. After the teeth begin to cut through the gums, often around the sixth month, thumb sucking is believed to be injurious. Most babies begin to ease up on the amount of their sucking before they have enough teeth for it to be really injurious.

There is no doubt that continued, steady thumb sucking well on into childhood does have some effect upon jaw shape. Does it cause the teeth to protrude? That depends to some extent upon the *kind* of sucking the child does. Some children actually pull their thumbs out of their mouths while they suck. This is bound to affect the shape of the jaw. But other children just seem to suck lightly on their thumbs, so that the shape is hardly affected.

Night sucking

My daughter, who is nearly 4, never sucks her thumb during the day. But just as soon as she goes to bed, she puts her thumb into her mouth and starts to suck. I find her with it in her mouth even when she is asleep. How can I break this habit?

WHY not try letting your daughter take her favorite toy to bed with her? Suggest that she hold this toy in her arm to "keep it warm." If you keep her hands busy with the toy, there is less chance that the thumb will find its way into her mouth. If this little trick does not work, I suggest that you see your doctor. He may be able to find the cause back of this night sucking. If it should come from over-fatigue in your child, the doctor would recommend a change in the bedtime schedule.

Mouth shape

I have heard that a badly shaped mouth always means that the person has been a thumb-sucker. Is this true?

THERE is not yet enough medical evidence to prove or disprove this claim. Some badly shaped jaws result from heredity. Others come from poor nutrition in either the prenatal stage or early infancy, when the bones of the jaws are still soft and easily put out of shape. Most badly formed jaws, however, are due to thumb sucking that persists after the teeth have cut through. This is especially true when the teeth protrude. If the teeth are merely crooked and seem to overlap each other, it generally means that the teeth are too large for the jaws. This is an inherited condition, not related to thumb sucking.

Sign of immaturity

Is thumb sucking in a school child a sign of immaturity?

IT MAY be, but not always. Many under-developed children suck their thumbs, but many show their immaturity in other ways. It is certainly a fact that a school age child is too old to suck his thumb. This form of behavior is one we associate with younger children or even with babies. The thumb-sucker is likely to get the reputation among his classmates of being a "baby," even though he is up to their level of development in other areas of his behavior. To avoid such a reputation, it is wise to encourage him to give up the thumb sucking habit as soon as possible.

Bitter tastes on thumb

When I was a child, my mother painted my thumb with iodine to prevent my sucking it. I have noticed a number of ads for different kinds of chemicals to use on a child's thumb to prevent thumb sucking. Are these safe? Do they work?

Any chemical endorsed by the American Medical Association, *Good Housekeeping*, or *Parents' Magazine* is perfectly safe to use on a child's thumb, except when he suffers from an allergy. Before using a chemical, it's wise to check with your doctor to make sure the one you use will be safe for *your* child.

As to how *effective* they are, that is a different story. In some cases, they work. In others, they do not. When the habit of thumb sucking is not too strong, and when the need for sucking is mainly outgrown, the child usually gives up thumb sucking soon after you start using the chemical. In most cases, however, the results are not so satisfactory. The child may not suck while the chemical is on his thumb, but it wears off in time. You have to renew it regularly, otherwise its effectiveness is lost.

Sign of poor adjustment

When a child sucks his thumb, does this mean that he is poorly adjusted?

Thumb sucking is not a foolproof sign of poor adjustment. It may have started at an earlier age when the child was poorly adjusted. But, because it developed into a habit from constant repetition, it may have persisted long after the poor adjustment was cleared up. It is true, however, that most people link thumb sucking with poor adjustment when they see it in a child past the age of 2 or 3 years.

chapter 9

Toilet training

Today's parents fuss much more about toilet training than did parents of past generations. The result is that for today's babies, toilet training is harder than it was for babies of earlier generations—and harder than it need be.

Why some parents worry

But why is there so much concern? Unfortunately, many parents have accepted the idea that a child's intelligence goes hand in hand with his rate of toilet training. They think that the brighter the child, the sooner he will be toilet trained. This notion is the main reason why parents worry about the age at which their babies can control bowels and bladders.

How important is intelligence?

It is true that the level of a child's intelligence has a bearing on the age he will learn to control his muscles. Toilet training, like sitting and standing, is a matter of muscular control. But it is also true that among babies of the *same* intelligence level, there are wide differences in the age when they learn control.

So intelligence is only *one* factor to consider. Other things are important, too, and one of the most important is emotional tension.

Paul and Eric are babies who are equal in mental ability. Yet they will be toilet trained at different ages. The difference will be even greater if their parents' attitudes are different. For example: Paul's parents feel calm and confident about toilet training. "No need to rush nature," they say. But Eric's parents make an issue about the matter. His older brothers and sisters tease and scold him because he "wets himself." These emotional tensions will delay Eric's toilet control.

Parents' attitude makes a difference

Another important thing to consider is the child's "readiness." As his body grows, he learns to control his *large* muscles *before* he controls his small muscles. You have noticed how a baby can use his arms to grasp *before* he can use his fingers to pick up small objects. Also, he can sit or stand before he can step with his feet. Now the urinary bladder and intestines are controlled by teams of *small muscles*. We have to wait, therefore, for signs that the baby is "ready" before we try to toilet train him.

A child must be mature enough

When is he ready?

How can you tell when a baby is ready for toilet training? Although there is no *sure* way, here is a simple method to use. Keep as accurate a record as possible of the times of day when your baby wets or soils his diapers. Do this for a week and see if there is any sign that a time pattern is taking form. Does he wet at about the same time every morning, afternoon, and evening? Does he soil his diapers at about the same times? When you see a consistent pattern, it shows his readiness for toilet training.

Be sure the child is ready

If there is no consistent pattern, drop the matter for a month, then test again. Don't try to toilet train your baby until you feel sure that he is ready. And don't persist in the training if you find out later that you guessed wrong about his being ready. It is bad for a child at any age to try to force him to learn something before he is ready to learn.

In this area of development, as in any other, no two babies are alike. Yet it often helps to know at about what age it is wise to test his readiness for toilet training. To give you a clue as to when to start, check the following average ages.

But remember that they are *averages*—and we can't expect averages to fit any one particular case perfectly.

> Bowel control ....12 to 18 months
> Bladder control during day...18 to 24 months
> Bladder control during night..34 to 40 months

A month or two before these dates, you might test your baby's readiness for training by the method I have suggested. If you find it is too early, drop the training for a month and try again later. Of course, you may find your baby's elimination is following a fairly regular pattern *before* these average dates. In that case, try the readiness test right then and there, without waiting for him to reach the age that fits the average baby.

Training is easy

Once you feel sure your baby is ready to be trained, start. This is very simple. At the times of day when he is used to wetting or soiling his diapers, put him on the "toidy seat" that you have fastened to the regular toilet. It's better to put him there 5 or 10 minutes ahead of the time he usually wets or soils his diapers. This helps him get used to the toidy seat. Besides, he may be a bit ahead of schedule.

For the first few days he may find this a slightly frightening or unusual experience. Don't worry. Babies adjust to new situations quickly. Chances are that your baby will find it as easy as other babies do.

The first few days

It's a good idea to stay with him at first until he gets used to the seat. After a day or two, this will not be necessary. And then it would be better to leave him alone, so he can concentrate on what he is there for. As soon as you start his training, be consistent about it—even if it means sacrificing some of your plans. You have to keep a baby on a regular schedule while the training is going on if you expect good results.

Here are three valuable aids to successful toilet training:

Three suggestions

1. Put some of the responsibility for it on the *baby's* shoulders. Teach him simple words like "Wee-wee" for urination and "Bow" for bowel movement. Encourage him to tell you when he wants to go to the toilet.

2. Put a stool in front of the toilet so he can go without your aid.

3. Use "training panties" during the day instead of

diapers. A few experiences of wet, cold panties will usually be enough to inspire his foresight.

The problem of
night training

Is it wise to wake a child to take him to the toilet at night? I doubt it. Night training takes longer than day training. Getting him up from a deep sleep to put him on the toilet often breaks his sleep and makes it hard for him to fall asleep again. Do it only if your doctor recommends it. In time, your child's muscles will become stronger and better controlled. Then he will be able to go through the night without having to go to the toilet.

Poor training

*My son is now 3 years old but he is far from being as well
trained as he was when I first began training him. What is wrong?*

IF YOUR child seems perfectly normal, both physically and mentally, look for the cause of the trouble in the training methods you have used. Perhaps you have not been consistent enough in forming habits of going to the toilet at set times, such as when he gets up from sleep, before and after meals, and when he comes home from play. It may be that your son suffers from emotional tenseness brought on by his feelings that he is just not measuring up. These feelings may be due to the worry you have shown about his lack of training. They may come from the fact that you are expecting more of him than he is able to do at his age. Try out the different possible causes of your failure. If you cannot solve the problem yourself, ask your doctor for help.

Toidy seat

In training a baby, is it necessary to use a regular training seat?

MOST toilets are too large for a baby or a young child. To use one, he would have to be held. This is not a good idea as it does not let him relax enough to function properly. Until your child's body is large enough to sit on a regular toilet seat comfortably, you should have a toidy seat. Take it with you when you go away from home with him, otherwise he is likely to have wet panties. Toidy seats fold up so you can carry them conveniently in a knitting bag.

Artificial aids

*My friends train their children by using glycerine suppositories
for regular bowel movements and by pouring warm
water over the genitals for urination. Should these be used?*

Most doctors today say that artificial aids should not be used. It is better to let nature take its own course. Artificial aids are likely to frighten a little child and build resistance toward the toilet. It takes time to train a child. You won't shorten the time if you create emotional tension.

Reaction to failure

*My mother told me that we were always spanked when we wet or
soiled ourselves. Does this help to train a young child?*

No, it does not. Spanking a child for failure to use the toilet *slows down* toilet training. First, spanking leads to nervous tension, and this conflicts with the relaxation a child needs to urinate or to move the bowels. Second, spanking often builds up a resisting attitude toward the whole toilet situation.

When your child has made a mistake, treat it in a matter-of-fact way. Say, "We won't bother this time, but the next time you feel you must go to the toilet, be sure to stop your play and go at once." When he lets you know he must go to the toilet, or when he goes by himself, *praise him* for it. *Your* calm confidence that he is learning and that he *can* learn will go a long way toward helping him to learn.

Jealousy

*My 3-year-old Tim was perfectly trained to keep dry during the
day—until his baby sister arrived two months ago. Now he is always wet,
and even when I put him on the toilet he does nothing. Why?*

Tim is suffering from jealousy of his new sister and is showing it by demanding attention from you by wetting his clothes. This is very common among young children.

Instead of putting emphasis on toilet training, it would be better if you devoted more of your time to your son. Make him feel that he is *not* being pushed into the background by his baby sister. Let him stay with you when you are doing things for the baby, and let him help whenever possible, even if he's more of a hindrance than a help. Give him as much time all alone with you as possible. When Tim again feels secure in your love, he will go back to his former schedule of training.

Fear of toilet

My daughter fusses and cries every time I put her on the toilet seat. How can I train her under such conditions?

Drop the training for another month, then try again. At that time, stay with your daughter when you put her on the toilet seat. It may take several days before she becomes used to the toilet. If she shows no signs of adjustment, it suggests that she is not yet ready to be trained. Drop the matter for another month or two and see how things are then. If she continues to protest for five or six months, ask your doctor about it.

Night training

My doctor advises against taking my child up at night for the toilet. Won't this lead to the habit of bed wetting?

Bed wetting does not result from letting a child sleep through. Follow your doctor's advice. I suggest, however, that you drop all liquids from your child's diet after 4 o'clock. Give him his milk in custard form, and avoid broth and soup in his supper. You might give him supper a little earlier so that he will have time after supper to let his food partially digest. Then, just before he is ready for bed, take him to the toilet. In time, this will be enough to guarantee a dry night.

Feeling of shame

My 8-year-old daughter wets her bed four or five nights a week. The older children tease her and this has made her very self-conscious and ashamed. How can I correct this situation?

First—and most important—you must put a stop to the teasing and ridicule of the older children. Next, talk plainly and sympathetically with your daughter. Explain that there is no need for worry, that she can learn to have a dry bed just as the other children have, and that you are going to help her.

Limit the liquids in her diet from 4 o'clock on, and explain why this is important. Then try to keep her as quiet and unexcited as possible in the evening. Don't allow radio listening, television watching, or playing active games. Let her read quietly if she wishes, but nothing exciting. Then, just before she goes to bed, give her the confidence that she will get through the night safely. Your attitude will go a long way toward helping her to lick this problem.

Bed Wetting

My 7-year-old Jimmie is a bed-wetter. I never had any
trouble with my two older children, both girls. Are boys
more likely to be bed-wetters than girls?

STUDIES of children show that boys are harder to toilet train than girls, and
that more boys suffer from bed wetting than girls. But boys become trained in
time, just as girls do. Perhaps you have not been as regular in training your son as
you were with your daughters. Or perhaps he is a more nervous, highstrung
child. Study him carefully to see if you can get any clues as to where the trouble
lies.

Excitement

Every time we go anywhere, my 5-year-old son wants to
go to the bathroom. This is often very embarrassing to us.
Is this the way all children behave?

MOST children your son's age have an urge to go to the bathroom when they
are excited. Remember that going to strange and different places is far more
exciting for a young child than it is for you. That is why he wants to go to the
bathroom. Don't let this embarrass you, for *your* tension will just increase *his*,
and then he is likely to wet himself. This will embarrass him to the point where
he may develop a real fear of going away from home.

chapter **10**

Understanding
your child

"Billie, I just don't understand why you do the things you do!"
"No, never mind the other children. It's your bedtime."
"You don't need a scooter, Sue. You have a wagon."
"Put away that silly gun and the rest of that foolish outfit."

How can a child be happy if he thinks people don't understand his reasons for doing certain things? Or if he believes they are treating him unfairly? How can he miss feeling like a martyr if his nearest and dearest misunderstand his wants and ambitions? Or if they joke about things that are close to his heart? *If a child is to be happy, he must feel that people understand him.*

Bonds between parent and child

IT IS a well-known fact that the ties or bonds between parent and child—so close in the early months of life—weaken as the child grows older. By the time the child reaches the teens, his relationship with his parents often resembles a battle. At the very time the child needs advice and guidance *most*, he refuses to turn to his mother and father. "They don't understand me," he explains.

And there is another trait that makes matters in the family circle even worse. Both young children and teen-agers often anger their parents by showing great respect for teachers or friends—and strong willingness to follow *their* advice instead of coming to parents for help. Youngsters don't do this to fan their parents' wrath! They do it because they have greater confidence in the understanding they get from *outsiders*. They feel their parents just don't understand as well.

Outsiders vs. parents

You want your child to grow up with a sincere belief in *your* ability to understand him. You want him to be willing to turn to *you* in times of crisis. Then it is up to you to build a relationship based on years of *mutual* understanding. It is just as important for him to understand *your* reasons for doing the things *you* do as it is for you to understand him!

Understanding works both ways

How to build understanding

UNDERSTANDING the wants, needs, and motives of people of widely different ages—that's not as easy as it may sound. First of all, you have to consider the difference in ages between you and your child. Remember: with age comes not only experience but also a growth in mental ability. Your child is not yet mature mentally. He can't think, reason, and remember as well as you can. He has not had the time or opportunity to build up the store of knowledge that you have. And he has not had the many and varied experiences of life you have had. We adults often forget this!

The child is still a child

Then, too, if you want to understand your child, you must always keep in mind the fact that we are living in a rapidly moving world. Things change over night. What worked when *you* were a child may be completely outworn by now. Ways of doing things, attitudes, beliefs—all are subject to change from one year to the next. Naturally your child will see things against the background of the present. You must learn to do this if you want to understand him. Each year he grows older and comes more and more in contact with people outside the home. That means he will be more and more influenced by *their* ways of thinking and doing, less and less by *your* ways.

Ours is a changing world

69

Try to recall how you felt about things when you were a child. That is the best way to understand a child. Only when you can do that can you hope to have a real understanding of your child, or of any child. Your childhood memories will, naturally, be vague and often incomplete. No matter, for the ones that really count—the pleasant or the heart-breaking experiences—will be vivid enough to help you imagine *how you would feel* if you were in your child's shoes.

Mothers have an advantage

The more experience you have had with children of all ages, either as an older sister or brother, baby sitter, teacher, or parent, the more understanding you will be. Why does a mother usually have more understanding of her children than a father does? Not because women are born with this ability, but because they have spent more time with children from the time they were young girls. Because of the mother's greater understanding of her children, the children generally prefer her to their father. Far too often fathers take this as a blow to their pride. They withdraw from their children, and this further decreases their ability to understand their children.

Study your child

To have a true understanding of your child, you must study him. He is much more complex than a complicated recipe in a cook book or a knotty problem in business. Watch his facial expressions. Notice the movements of his body. Listen attentively to what he says, and *how* he says it. Little

Actions may say more than words

children, especially, express their feelings and emotions more vividly through facial and body movements than through speech. Even when children have a good command of language, they often show how they feel about things through their facial expressions better than through what they say. Yes, it *is* well worth your time and effort to study your child carefully if you want to understand him.

Play fair!

It is important, too, to encourage your child to tell you *how he feels about things.* Don't ever make the mistake of letting him suspect that you are not in sympathy with what he tells you. Don't ridicule or tease him for what he tells you. And don't leave him with the impression that you are too busy to listen to him. Be fair: hear *his side* of the story before you draw your own conclusions about why he did what he did. Remember that a child is not an adult. You can't judge him by adult standards. You can't pin adult motives to his simple acts. If you want to have a real understanding of him, *learn to see things as he sees them.*

Upset by trifles

I have three children, ranging in age from 4 to 8 years. They are happy children but they all get very much upset by trifles, such as not getting mittens of the colors they want, or being just a few minutes late for a radio program they want to hear. Shouldn't I try to curb this trait?

I⟊ is unfortunate when people go through life being upset by "trifles." They make themselves, and everyone else, unhappy. But the things you, an adult, consider "trifles" are likely to be very important to your children! Perhaps they had their hearts set on hearing a certain program. You really cannot blame them for being upset when they miss part of it. To them this program is important, even if it seems unimportant to you, or less important than whatever they were doing that caused them to be late for it.

You can curb a child's tendency to be upset by trifles only if you can convince him that they *are* trifles and not worth the emotional energy he spends on them. Only as your children grow older and more mature in their outlook on life will they be able to see things in better balance or perspective. Then they will realize, as you do now, that some things are simply not worth getting upset about. You can help them get this outlook by showing them the merits and weaknesses of the things they now regard as so terribly important.

Father's intolerance

My husband is very intolerant of our children's noisy laughter and sloppiness. He says they should be quiet at the table, have good manners, and be well groomed. But I feel that children should be natural, and it isn't natural for children to be perfect ladies and gentlemen. Who is right?

You and your husband are both partly right and partly wrong. Of course we should not expect them to be "perfect ladies and gentlemen." Perfection in any line takes years to achieve, if it is *ever* achieved. And yet you shouldn't expect *too little* of the children. Your husband is going to the opposite extreme because he doesn't understand that children are children, not adults. Both of you should discuss what your children are capable of, set reasonable standards for them, and then expect them to come up to those standards.

Your point of view will keep your children from achieving what they are capable of. *Your husband's* will discourage them, so they will not try to do even what they can do. Try to hit a happy medium.

Food dislikes

> *I simply cannot understand why my children have such strong dislikes for some of the foods my husband and I enjoy. It makes preparation of the meals very hard for me.*

You would understand your children's attitudes toward the foods you and your husband enjoy if you realized that children are children, not adults. The food likes of children and adults are different because children have a keener sense of smell and taste than adults have. That is why many of the foods adults like, especially highly seasoned ones, really do "bite the tongue" of a child and make him dislike those foods. Why not ask your children why they do not like certain foods? Then you will understand their reactions better.

Remembering instructions

> *Frank, my 6-year-old, seems to let my instructions go in one ear and out the other. If I ask him to pick up his things or bring me something from upstairs, he forgets all about it. Why?*

A child's memory is not an adult's memory, you must realize. The things you ask Frank to do are not of personal interest to him. He has very little *need* to remember, therefore. This is true of adults, too, but to a far less degree than of children. The next time you ask your son to do something for you, ask him to repeat your request. This will help him to pay closer attention to what you have asked him to do for you. It should help him to remember better.

Carelessness

> *My children, 3- and 5-years old, are very careless with their toys. They are constantly breaking them because they do not take proper care of them. Are all children careless?*

All young children are careless until they learn the importance of proper care. This is something you must teach your children. They do not understand that toys, clothes, and other articles are easily broken by careless handling. Only after repeated experiences of having fond possessions broken or spoiled can they see the connection between the way they handle things and the condition of the articles. Then they begin to understand that they must handle things more carefully if they don't want to ruin them.

chapter 11

What is personality?

Is personality something a child either has or doesn't have? Most people seem to think so. They believe personality is something a child is born with, and that if he is lucky he will be gifted with the ability to "win friends and influence people" from the moment he is a tiny tot in his cradle.

Nothing is further from the truth! A person is *not* born with a personality. He *acquires* one as he goes through life—much as he develops the ability to read or to play the piano. True, he inherits the *foundation* of his personality, in the form of physical and mental capacities—but the *pattern* of his personality is built up as he goes through life.

Personality develops as time goes on

And personality is not something definite like height or weight. Rather, it consists of all the personal qualities that make each person different from every other person. It is a *general quality of behavior* that is influenced by a central "core." This core is the person's own idea or picture of what he is and what he can do. He doesn't inherit this core of his personality. He *develops* it from the way he is treated by other people from the moment he is born.

73

Can personality be changed?

PERSONALITY begins to develop so early in life—even before the child is born—that we often think it is inherited and that there is therefore nothing we can do to improve it. If this were true, parents would just sit back and do nothing, thus hurting their children's future happiness and success. Fortunately, we *can* improve personalities. We *can* correct many of the personality patterns that start off badly if we recognize them in time, and if we make a strong, persistent effort to correct them before they become too deep-rooted.

Personalities can be improved

But this means we must start early. The important time to mold personality is during the early years of life—before the child starts school, when his contacts are mainly with members of his own immediate family. Since this is so, parents must realize one of their most important duties and responsibilities —guiding a child's development in such a way that he will be guaranteed a personality that will be an asset, not a handicap, the rest of his life.

How the child sees himself is important

THE quality of a person's behavior—which, after all, is the basis on which others judge his behavior—is a direct reflection of what that person thinks of himself in relation to other people. What your child thinks of himself will reflect what *you* think of him during the early formative years of his life. Suppose, for example, that *you* think he is the most important person in your world and you allow him to do as he pleases, when and how he pleases. Is it *his* fault if, later on, people label him a "spoiled brat" and other children do not want to play with him?

How "spoiled brats" are born

It is hard to change a child's attitude about himself, once it is established. You may find, for instance, that your child thinks of himself as more important than anyone else thinks he is. Or he may think he has far less ability than other children when, actually, he has no real ground for this belief. Then it is up to you, his parents, to help him to get a truer picture of himself than he now has. The sooner you do this, the easier it will be to offset the false impression he has.

74

To repeat, the core of a child's personality—what he thinks of himself as an individual—comes from his early experiences. Never make the mistake of thinking that the experiences of the first few years of a child's life "don't count" just because you see no signs that he has *conscious* memories of those experiences. It is true that, as he grows older, he will not remember much of what happened to him during the first two or three years of his life. But those early experiences, pleasant and unpleasant, frightening and comforting, are stored away in his *subconscious mind*. They are not forgotten.

A child's mind is a storehouse

These experiences affect his conscious thought in a way that is hard to put your finger on. Take the timid, fearful child, afraid to do what other children do. What holds him back, usually, is his subconscious memory of frightening experiences in his early years. The influence of these early happenings is often hard to detect as he grows older and shows no trace of remembering them. Yet they may lie at the root of his timidity.

Personality traits may be traced far back

Building healthy personalities

To BUILD a healthy personality, parents must supply their child with an environment that promotes feelings of being secure, loved, and wanted. They must see to it that the ideas he develops about himself while he is still at home with the family will be equally as serviceable when he leaves home for the broader world of neighborhood, school, and community. Also, they should see to it that the associations outside the home are of the right type, the kind that influence the child's personality favorably. During these early formative years, it is far better in the long run for a child to have no companionship outside the home than to have companionship of the kind that will leave an unfavorable mark on his whole personality pattern.

Foundations of a healthy personality

Laying the foundations of a child's personality is mainly a *home* responsibility. That is why it is important that you consider thoughtfully the kind of personality you want your child to have. Naturally, you want him to have a "nice" personality, to be liked by people of all ages, and to be happy. Whether you achieve this goal or not will depend on how much time, effort, and consistent training you put into your job.

This thing called personality is too serious a matter to leave to chance or to the *hope* that the child will mold his own personality. From your own more mature experience, *you* know far better than he what kinds of personality patterns help a person to get along successfully in the world. This is one of the most important obligations of parenthood. In fairness to your child, you should not shirk it.

Importance of parents

Just how important are parents in the formation of a child's personality?

Parents are important in two ways. *First,* they contribute to the child the physical and mental characteristics on which the child's personality will later develop. *Second,* they are important during the child's early years when his personality is being formed and he has no other model to copy. He imitates the personality traits he observes in his parents.

Of equal importance, his parents are the ones who are chiefly responsible for what the child thinks of himself, and for the picture he has of himself as a person. How he will act when he goes outside the home, into the broader world of people, will depend largely upon what he has learned to think about himself as a person when he was still young and his social contacts were largely those of his immediate family.

Importance of playmates

If playmates are important in forming a child's personality, shouldn't parents be very careful about the sort of children their child goes with?

Parents should be careful not only of the type of children their child associates with, but also of the type of adult the child is with. A baby sitter, for example, may very easily do far more harm than a parent realizes, even though she is with the young child for only a short time on rare occasions. For one thing, the sitter may use fear as a method of making the child behave. This may lead to fears even when the sitter is not there, and develop in the child a timidity he would not have learned if it were not for the baby sitter's methods. Teachers, who spend so much time with children, are powerful forces for good or bad in the child's personality development.

The child is so anxious to be liked by those of his own age, and to be included in their play groups, that the children he is with are very powerful forces in the development of his personality. Each year, as he grows older, the influence of his associates outside the home increases. And each year, the children he plays with exert a greater influence over him than they did the year before. Because this is so, it is very important that parents see to it that their child's companions are of the sort they would like their child to be. This is especially true of the child's most intimate friends. They are the ones with whom he will spend the major part of his play time. And they are the ones he will be most anxious to be accepted by.

Desirable traits

What personality traits should parents try to develop in their children?

THIS is a big question to answer. Besides, it cannot be answered for every child in the same way, because each one is an individual. Each one should cultivate traits in keeping with his own individual nature.

There are, however, certain personality traits that are universally found in people who are well liked and successful in life. These are the traits that every parent should strive to cultivate in a child. They include good sportsmanship, generosity, truthfulness, honesty, interest in others, unselfishness, cooperativeness, and initiative. The well-adjusted, successful, happy person is one who thinks more of others than of himself, lets others know how he feels instead of bottling it up inside, and is willing to submerge his own personal interests in those of the group. In general, he is an extrovert rather than an introvert—he is more outgoing, less self-interested.

Personality changes

Is it true that a child's personality changes early in adolescence when he develops into an adult?

THE personality of a child is set during the early years of childhood. It changes little as the child moves into adolescence if he is not anxious to change and if he is not willing to put the necessary effort into making the change. Even if he has the will, he may not know how to go about it without professional advice and help.

Most boys and girls do not change their personalities as they change from children into men and women. On the contrary, the personality pattern they developed as children becomes more and more firmly set as time passes. Any

77

change that does take place is in the direction of the trait already present. In other words, if he was selfish as a child, he is likely to become more selfish as an adolescent. Perhaps he will be more subtle or clever in the way he expresses his selfishness, but he will still be selfish. In the same way, a child who was a good sport, win or lose, will continue to be a good sport as he grows older. He will not suddenly turn into a poor sport just because his body has changed.

I know it would be comforting to think that a child will leave behind him all his bad traits when he emerges from childhood into adolescence. Unfortunately, things just don't work that way!

Correcting bad habits

What is the best way to correct a bad personality trait, such as selfishness?

AN unpleasant personality trait is a signal that something is wrong in your child's world. He has a basic need that he is trying to satisfy in the wrong way. Before you can help him, you must find out what this need is. Then you can help him learn to find satisfaction in a more wholesome manner. A selfish child, for example, is so full of his own need to feel secure and important that he does not consider the needs of others. He wants the largest piece of cake, more than his share of turns on a swing.

But like all children, the selfish child also wants the love and approval of his parents and the friendship of his playmates. You can help him find out that sharing, not selfishness, will bring him this deeper security. Little by little, he will begin to understand that sharing brings him love, approval, and friends and that these are more satisfying than anything he can get by selfishness. Then one day, he will find a deeper joy in sharing, an unselfish joy that springs from the pleasure he has given to someone else.

chapter **12**

Obedience

Cᴀɴ parents expect perfect obedience from children? No:
learning to conform to rules and regulations is a long, hard
process—much more so than most adults realize. If the child
shows *some* improvement from year to year, and if he shows
a willing, cooperative attitude, be satisfied. That is as much
as you can expect.

What learning to obey means

Lᴇᴀʀɴɪɴɢ to be obedient means four separate, distinct
things: (1) *understanding* rules and regulations, and knowing
when and how to apply them; (2) *remembering* these rules
and regulations; (3) *ability to tie up* these rules with any
situation that may arise (especially difficult if the new situation isn't like any the child has previously experienced); and
(4) *willingness* of the child to conform to the rules because he
realizes they are right or that it will be to his personal advantage to do so.

79

Learning is a slow process

I<small>N</small> childhood all learning is slow because the child has no ready-made basis or foundation on which to build. Rules are far too often just words to a child, vague words that have no real meaning for him, and are therefore hard to learn. How, then, can you expect him to remember them when even things that do have meaning are so easily forgotten?

Don't expect too much too soon

The best policy to follow is to take it easy with discipline —if you want good results and a healthy attitude in your child toward rules, people in authority, and conformity to a socially acceptable pattern of behavior. Go slow on the punishment, be free with your praise and approval. Above all, try to be patient and tolerant with mistakes. Don't allow yourself to become upset or embarrassed when your child misbehaves in public. And don't allow yourself to feel that you are a failure as a parent just because your child is not a model of obedience.

Don't force behavior pattern too soon

It may be comforting to you to know that the "good" little boys and girls who never caused their parents any trouble are too often, as they grow older, the very ones who bring heartaches to their parents. The reason is clear. Having been forced into a pattern of behavior too mature for their childish years, they later rebel and go to the opposite extreme. They develop into "problem cases," or build up an attitude of deep resentment against those who are responsible for making them too "good" for their own good. In the long run, then, it is the parent who pays the penalty for expecting too much at too early an age.

How to develop desirable obedience

H<small>ERE</small> are some ways a parent can help the child to learn to be obedient without the harmful aftermath that comes with forcing him to be too obedient too soon:

Make sure he understands

1. *Explain* each new rule you make to your child in words he can understand. Then, to make sure that he does understand, ask him to tell you what the rule means *to him*. In this way you can quickly clear up any misunderstanding he may have.

2. Give him a chance to learn to *apply* the rule to as many different situations as possible so that you can show him the similarity in each situation. If you are trying to teach him to

be courteous to older people, show him what you mean by "older people" by explaining that Grandmother is an older person, and his teacher is an older person. You cannot expect him, with his limited experience, to be able to make these comparisons himself.

Show him how to apply your rules

3. Teach him *one new rule at a time,* and don't try to teach another rule until you are sure he has mastered the first one. Piling one rule on top of the other merely confuses a child and defeats its own end.

4. Be *consistent* in your rules for right and wrong, for what he may do or may not do. Remember: it is hard for a child to learn to do what you want him to do. Don't make the learning harder for him by confusing him, as you are bound to if you lead him to believe that something is wrong today and then, tomorrow, you shut your eyes to the very thing you made such an issue of the day before!

Avoid zigzags

5. Be *tolerant* of his slips. Don't assume they were intentional. Even as an adult, don't you sometimes make mistakes? So why expect *him* to be perfect? A slip on his part means he has not mastered the rule completely. He needs more time to learn it and more explanation from you so that he can understand exactly what the rule means and how to apply it to different situations.

6. Encourage your child by *praising* him for his efforts to do what you ask him to do—even if his efforts fall short of your expectations. You must make it worth his while to try to be good, or he will take the line of least resistance and do what he wants to do. When following a rule has been especially hard for him, give him a reward in the form of some special treat or privilege. This is not a bribe. It is a token of your appreciation for his efforts.

Give rewards, not bribes

7. *Use punishment sparingly.* It is fair to punish a child only when it is clear that he both knows what he has done is wrong and has intentionally defied your instructions. Then, and then only, are you being fair to him by punishing him.

8. *Keep calm* and take an impersonal, objective attitude toward discipline. Never let a child feel that your punishment is a form of revenge, or that you are trying to get even with him. Instead, take the attitude that "This is wrong because people believe it is wrong," not just because you, his parent, say it is wrong. Many young children, and many teen-agers, become balky and contrary when they feel that obedience is merely a whim on the part of the parent.

Naughtiness in public

> *My 4-year-old is a good child at home but he always makes a scene*
> *or does something naughty in public. I hate to punish him*
> *as it makes me feel conspicuous and embarrassed. Am I wrong?*

CHANCES are that the people who see your son misbehave wonder what sort of mother you are when you allow him to misbehave without some form of reprimand. This, it seems to me, should be more embarrassing to you than to punish your child. You do not have to create a scene to be firm, but you should let your son know that you will not stand for his cutting-up as a means of bossing you just because you are in public. If you believe his misbehavior stems from fatigue or overexcitement, take him home at once, no matter how inconvenient this may be. A tired or excited child cannot help being troublesome and it is not fair, under such conditions, to treat his misbehavior as intentional.

Obedience to outsiders

> *When my husband and I go out, we employ a high school girl*
> *as a sitter. Our children, ages 6, 4, and 1, are very troublesome and*
> *simply won't obey her. Even the baby tries to do as he pleases.*
> *Shouldn't children obey others than their parents?*

YES, a child should, of course, obey anyone in authority. But, when a child recognizes that the person in authority is just a trifle older than he, he is likely to try to take advantage of that person. This is especially true of a young, inexperienced girl. From every angle—safety, discipline, and appreciation of the importance of routine—I think you would be far better off to get an older and more experienced person to stay with your children when you are out. The children are far more likely to obey an older person than a young girl. Then you will not have the problem of losing the effects of your discipline every time you turn your children over to the care of this young baby sitter.

Resistance to discipline

> *My 4-year-old daughter rebels against anything and everything*
> *I tell her to do. She seems to take delight in breaking all the rules. The*
> *more I punish her, the worse she seems to be. Why?*

CHILDREN the age of your daughter are likely to resist authority and to try to assert their independence. But, when the resistance is very marked, as in the case of your daughter, it usually means too strict discipline for the child's age and level of development. In the future, try to allow your daughter to make some of her decisions for herself and to take more initiative. Except when she might actually hurt herself, let her learn by stubbing her toes and burning her fingers. There is no quicker way of breaking down the stubborn, resisting attitude of a child than to let the child suffer the consequences of his or her mistakes. Don't be too protective. Your child will resent it and will make a point of resisting everything you want her to do.

Spanking

We were spanked as children when we misbehaved. But my friends tell me spanking is old-fashioned and that it is bad for a child's personality. Is this the modern point of view?

YES, spanking as a regular punishment for any kind of misbehavior is definitely regarded as "old-fashioned." The reason it is not widely used today is that it does not serve its purpose as well as other forms of punishment do. You can, of course, make a child afraid by sound spankings, but at the same time you are likely to turn him into a sneak and liar. Furthermore, spanking has no educational value. By being spanked, a child does not learn *why* what he did was wrong or *what* he should have done instead. Besides, the punisher usually gives the spanking when he is angry. Is it surprising, under such conditions, that the child interprets this to mean that the person is very angry and no longer loves him? Of course all these effects of spanking leave an unfavorable mark on the child's personality.

Praise

I have always felt that praising children would make them conceited and, as a result, they would not try to do what they are supposed to do. Am I wrong?

IF YOU praise the child's *acts* instead of the child himself, there is no cause for alarm about making the child conceited. It sounds like a trivial shade of difference to an adult but, to a child, there is a great difference in meaning. He focuses his attention on what he has done, if that is what is being praised, and does not think in terms of himself. As a result, it will not make him conceited and indifferent. Studies of praise have shown that children of all ages respond favorably to praise and try to do what is asked of them far more eagerly than when they are scolded or punished.

Putting to bed

When my 6-year-old son is naughty, I send him to bed.
Is this a good way to get obedience?

IT IS a good way to get obedience only if you stress the fact that he must be very tired or otherwise he would not be so naughty. The important thing is not to associate bed with punishment in the child's mind. Otherwise, you are likely to create in him a serious rebellion against going to bed.

Strict discipline

My husband expects our children to jump at his word, and to be
as polite as the average adult. When I tell him they are too
young to behave like adults, he insists that if they don't learn
to be obedient when they are young, we will have a lot of
trouble with them when they are teen-agers. Who is right?

YOU are right and your husband is wrong about this matter. I am sure you are showing a far better understanding of your children's capacities than he is.

Your husband's idea that strict adherence to rules now instead of greater freedom will make your children less troublesome as teen-agers, is wrong. It usually works in just the opposite way! The stricter the discipline, the more rebellious the child becomes, and the harder he is to handle later on. As a result of strict discipline, many children become so contrary in their attitudes as they grow older that they do just the opposite of what they are supposed to do. It's a way of asserting their independence.

Age of obedience

At what age can a parent reasonably expect a child to be obedient?

YOU cannot put an age limit on obedience. Some children are obedient far earlier than others. It may be because they have a different personality pattern, or because they have learned from past experience that it is to their personal advantage to be obedient, or because they are afraid to be anything but obedient. For the average child in America today, you can expect the child to be reasonably obedient when he is 6 or 7 years old. Then, for a few years he is likely to go into a tail spin and be quite disobedient and openly defiant of all rules. In the early teens, he comes back into the family fold and begins to act as his parents expect him to act.

Anger and discipline

I find it very difficult to control my temper when my children misbehave. Does this break down the effects of my discipline?

For good discipline you must learn to keep calm and unruffled. Otherwise, the child will become excited, too, and will do many things he would not otherwise do. Besides, when you become angry, the discipline loses much of its force because the child interprets it to mean an expression of anger on your part, not a scolding or punishment he himself has earned for his misbehavior. Learn to count to 10 or even 20 before saying anything when your child is especially exasperating. By then you will have calmed down and can handle the situation better.

chapter **13**

Helping your child overcome fears

Every child is afraid of something at some time or other. *How many* fears he has, and how severe they are, usually depends upon the people he grows up with, especially during the early years of his life. Like mannerisms and speech, children learn fears partly by imitation and partly by association.

Most fears are not inherited— they're learned

True, nature provides some fears, especially those that prevent the child from harming himself. Fear of falling is an example. But only few of the fears of children in our modern world have been inherited. Most of them have been *learned* as the child lives with people who show similar fears or who instill in him the need for caution.

How fears grow

"Be careful!" "Watch out!" "Don't touch—it will hurt you!" Constant warnings—and seeing other children show fears —build up a child's fears. Even adults are sometimes to blame for giving him a model for fear. Mother or the baby sitter may turn her head away at a flash of lightning, or cover her ears at a clap of thunder. Perhaps she says, "I'm afraid to do it." In this way she sets a pattern which the child follows even though he may not know the reason for the fear the adult is experiencing.

Then, too, the growing child will remember past experiences that were painful or terrifying. He will try to avoid similar experiences with situations that resemble the unpleasant one. In this way, fears spread as time passes. Many more are built up than are actually necessary or even useful to the child.

How fears grow

The good and the bad in fear

Are all fears bad? No, some are necessary and useful. Without them, the child would "dash in where angels fear to tread," and harm himself.

Some fears are good

Some fears are reasonable: fears of high places that are not properly protected and of animals in cages which look harmless enough but which can be ferocious if teased. Such fears can protect a child from hurt.

But fears seldom are limited to these *protective* ones. Far too often the child develops fears of people, animals, and situations for which there is absolutely no need for fear. As a result, he not only makes himself unhappy but he often cuts himself off from experiences that would otherwise be pleasant and profitable. These are the fears which are totally unnecessary and which, if allowed to persist, will prove to be great handicaps throughout his life.

When a child is timid and frightened of anything and everything, it means that he is suffering from feelings of insecurity. This is not *his* fault. He has been *made* that way by people who have tried to protect him from the hurts and bruises which are a normal part of every child's life. Parents, grandparents, brothers and sisters, or others usually are responsible.

Overprotection may cause fear

A sensible approach

I am not suggesting that we should permit a child to be foolhardy, or encourage him to take unnecessary chances. I *am* suggesting that we should avoid protecting him so closely that he loses confidence in himself and feels afraid of anything and everything that is new or different. Reasonable precautions are necessary—but unreasonable restraints and warnings are sure to turn a potentially successful person into a timid, cowardly one.

The dangers of fear

When a child is permitted to grow up in the clutches of fear, he will never be happy. Nor will he ever accomplish as much as his natural abilities would otherwise permit. His personality will be warped, he will have unwholesome attitudes toward life, and he will live a life which is as unsatisfactory to everyone he meets as it is to him.

How can we free a child from unnecessary fear yet, at the same time, help him to learn to be afraid of things which he should fear for his own safety? This is a difficult task, I know, but it's a very necessary one.

Two suggestions

First: parents and all who come in close contact with a child need to be always on guard lest unnecessary fears develop in him. Second—and of even greater importance: learn to spot the *budding* of fears which, when in full bloom, may be very difficult to get rid of. It is just as wrong to encourage a child to have no fears as it is to encourage too many fears. A happy balance between these two extremes should be the goal of all of us who are responsible for guiding a child's life.

Useful fears

Are there any fears that are necessary and useful—and what are they?

Yes, there are times when fear is both useful and necessary. Fear can be a danger signal to warn the child of approaching danger. Take the child who has been encouraged to show *no* fear of animals. He may receive scars that will permanently disfigure his face if he ignores the growls of an otherwise friendly dog chewing on a bone. And the foolhardy one who prides himself on being afraid of nothing could easily fall to his death while climbing on a roof to show his more timid companions "how easy it is."

I believe the important thing is to train the child to be *cautious* in the face of possible dangers, but not to fear things that are perfectly harmless. Of course, a child has not had enough knowledge and experience to see this difference. So it's the responsibility of his parents, teachers, and all who take care of him to label things "dangerous" or "safe" for him. And we also have to teach him *how* he can learn this difference for himself as he grows older and his experience broadens.

Harmful fears

What fears are harmful and destructive? What should a parent do to avoid allowing such fears to get a strong hold on a child?

Fears that are harmful and destructive are the purely imaginary ones. Fears that are *real*, however, act as danger signals that serve useful purposes. Besides, *real* fears can be brought out in the open, discussed, and thus can be understood by the child.

You can't do that with imaginary fears. These are the fears that come from stories the child has heard or read, from comic books, radio or television programs, or moving pictures. Or they may come from adults or other children who try to control his behavior by threats of possible danger if he does not do as they say. Such fears exist only in the child's mind. They cannot be brought out in the open. As a result, the more he thinks about them, the stronger they are likely to become.

Dealing with imaginary fears is never easy because it is hard for a parent to know what they are. However, with a young child, it is possible to get him to talk about his imaginary experiences by encouraging rather than discouraging him. Once he brings these fears out in the open and tells you what they are, it is always possible to show the child how unlikely it is for the thing he fears to ever affect him in any way. But don't make the mistake of ridiculing the child's imaginary fears. If you do, you block your one avenue of approach to such fears. You will have no way of knowing what they are.

Imaginary fears

How do imaginary fears get started? Does the child just make them up, or does he get them from his playmates?

Even an imaginary experience must have some roots in reality. A child just cannot imagine something he has never experienced before in some form. Sometimes, but not always, he may pick up his imaginary fears from his playmates. Most imaginary fears come from the stories a child hears and, later, when he is older, reads for himself—from radio or television programs—from comic books—from moving pictures—even from adults who try to control his behavior by threats of possible dangers if he doesn't do as he is told.

We adults can see a fanciful movie with trees suddenly turning into people and reaching out for a person who is walking through the woods—and it doesn't faze us. But not so with a child. He will accept such a moving picture as real, and he will likely be afraid to go near a tree in the future for fear it will suddenly turn into a person who will grab him off so that he can never return home.

Children don't have enough intelligence or experience to separate the real from the fanciful in what they see or hear. That is why it is most important for parents and teachers to *preview* the things a child sees, and to be on their guard about what he hears. I know that even the most watchful parent cannot keep a child from seeing and hearing *some* things which he will misinterpret and thus be afraid of. But, by reasonable care, you *can* prevent many potential fears of an imaginary sort. Follow the practice of talking things over with a child to encourage him to bring out into the open things which might be puzzling him or even terrifying him. Then chances are good that you can help him to reduce to a minimum the number and severity of his imaginary fears.

Fear of being left alone

> *My son, who is nearly 7 years old, is afraid to have me leave him alone even for an hour or two. Isn't he old enough to be left alone?*

No, if you mean going out of the house and leaving your son there. Naturally he is frightened at the prospect of being in the house alone, and this is a fear you should respect. If you are merely going to a neighbor's home where he could reach you quickly by opening the door or window and calling, that would be a different story. But leaving a child of 7 alone for an hour or more out of easy reach is not only a terrifying experience for a child—it is also a dangerous thing for you to do.

Separation fears

> *Because I must visit my sick mother in another town, my 4-year-old Linda has developed a fear that I will never return. Every time I go away, usually once a week, she gets very upset, eats and sleeps badly while I am gone, and clings to me while I am home. How can I overcome this fear?*

Once a fear has developed that a parent, especially the mother, will never return, the child is likely to behave as your daughter does. This is upsetting to you, especially when you know it is your duty to make frequent visits to your sick mother. And it is equally upsetting to the person who takes care of your child during your absence. So far as the child is concerned, I can assure you that she suffers more from this fear than you realize.

Here is a method which always works in a case like yours. Every time you leave your child alone in her room or in another part of the house while you attend to household duties, show her by the hands of the clock you have placed in her room just where the hands will be when you return. "When the big hand is here and the little hand is there, I'll be through with the dishes and will come back to you!" Then keep your word and be back on the dot. Call her attention to this by showing her the position of the hands of the clock.

Do the same with the calendar when you go away, and have the person who is in charge show her on the calendar what day it is when you are out of town. Telephone her every evening when you are away from home, telling her just when you will be back. Do this even if you are away from home for only part of the day. It means a lot to a child to be able to keep in contact with the mother, even by telephone, and it helps to reassure the child that the mother will return as she promised.

Fear of dark

My children have all been afraid of the dark. Is this true of most children or have I handled things in such a way as to make them afraid?

Fear of the dark is so common among children that few escape it. Never, under any circumstance, make a child feel ashamed or inadequate because of such fears. Calling him a "fraidy cat," for example, is cruel and unforgivable. Instead, respect his fear by letting him know you are *with* him not against him. When he is frightened, stay with him until his fear subsides. Permit him to have the door of his room open so he can hear the familiar sounds of the home. Leave a night light burning in his room or in the hall if he asks for it. Above all, let him know you will be within earshot and ready to come to him if he calls you.

When the dark is gone and the world bathed in sunshine, that is the psychological time to encourage a child to talk about his fears of the dark. Bringing the matter out into the open not only helps you to see what is frightening him but the very fact that he talks about his fears will make him realize that they are not so bad as they seemed when it was dark. Fears bottled up inside the child are likely to grow stronger and more terrifying as his imagination has a chance to exaggerate them beyond all reason.

Missing out

My daughter is always afraid she will not get her share of anything her sisters and brothers get. At birthdays or Christmas, for example, she will ask if the gifts she received from friends and relatives cost as much as those her brothers and sisters received. Isn't this a bad trait to allow to go on?

It is unfortunate that a child feels this way for it not only makes her unhappy but also makes her resentful against her brothers and sisters if she feels they are getting more than she does. While her emphasis is on the gifts, actually she is revealing that she is afraid she is not loved as much as her sisters and brothers. Try to find out why she feels this way. Does she get her full share of attention and praise from her family and friends? You know you love her, but make an extra effort to show it in ways she can understand. A trip or treat sometimes just for the two of you will help her feel special and wanted. As her self-confidence and assurance of being loved grows, she will learn not to equate love with presents and will gradually lose her fear of missing out on gifts.

Unpopularity

> My son has never been very popular with the boys. He is always
> saying he doesn't want to go here or there because he is afraid the boys
> won't want to play with him. How can I overcome his fear
> of not being liked by other people, especially the other boys?

FEAR of not being liked is a negative attitude that will get your son nowhere. You must try to replace it with a *positive* attitude in the form of a desire to be popular. Invite some of your son's playmates to your home and watch the children at play. Try to see what your son does that makes him unpopular. Then try to help him to develop good sportsmanship, cooperativeness, play skills, and other traits that are necessary to popularity among children. When your son begins to win friends, his fear of not being liked will disappear.

Being hurt

> My daughter, age 6 years, has been quite unhealthy. She has
> had several minor operations, countless visits to the doctor and
> dentist, and plenty of cuts and bruises. All of these have
> built up a fear of being hurt, with the result that she puts on a scene
> as soon as she steps inside a doctor's or dentist's office.

BEING hurt, either physically or emotionally, will leave scars that are hard to get rid of. Just telling your daughter to "keep her chin up" and "be brave" will not be enough. Try to convince her that temporary hurts are better than the greater hurts that will come if she refuses to let the doctor or dentist treat her. Furthermore, show her that if she relaxes, thinks about something else, and is cheerful, treatments will not seem so bad to her. As for the psychological hurts, such as injured feelings, try to make her see that people are not intentionally cruel. If she will only ignore things said or done that hurt her, people will not be offended or will not do anything in the future to hurt her. She must learn to be brave about these as about physical hurts.

Doing wrong thing

My child is so afraid she will do or say the wrong thing when she is out that it makes her self-conscious and nervous. She gets very upset every time she goes out. As a result, she doesn't like to go out with people.

ARE YOU sure you have not put so much stress on manners, on doing the socially *correct* thing, that you have fostered this fear in your child? Now it's up to you to try to undo the trouble you have caused. Emphasize that people rarely notice mistakes that others make, that no one is perfect, and that people make big allowances for the mistakes of children. Tell her also that if she will just relax and behave normally, she will be far less likely to do the wrong thing than if she allows herself to become tense and nervous. Send her off with a cheerful smile and the parting words, "Have a good time"—instead of a series of warnings about what to do and what not to do. *Your* attitude will go a long way toward making her confident that she can and will do the right thing.

Fear of death

How can a parent prevent a child from becoming afraid of death?

THE only way is to remove any unpleasant associations with death. Far too often, children are told by adults that, if they are not good now, they will be punished after they die and not allowed to go to Heaven. Some children are told that the body is "eaten up by worms" when it is buried. These associations naturally make the child afraid of death—not only for themselves but also for those they love. Added to the fear of what will happen to a person after death is the fear of what will happen to them if someone near and dear to them dies. Every child should be reassured, time after time, that if anything happens to his parents, Grandmother, or Aunt Nell, or some friend of the family will take care of him. This will do much to ease the tension that comes from such fears.

Worries

When does fear become a worry?
What is the difference between fear and worry?

MOST people use the words "fear" and "worry" as if they were the same, with worry being a mild fear. Actually, "fear" means an emotional state aroused by a *real* situation, person, or animal, while "worry" is an emotional state resulting from an imaginary situation, person, or animal. Worry is far more frequent in older children, adolescents, and adults than it is in younger children. Only when the child reaches the stage of mental ability when he can think and see beyond his nose is he subject to worry. Worry, like fear, is damaging to the physical and mental health of a person. For that reason, it is wise to encourage the child to talk freely about what worries him so you can show him how groundless most of his worries are. In addition, putting his worries into words will often help him to see for himself how foolish and how needless they are.

Fear of animals

My son, age 5, was badly clawed by a cat when he was younger. Now he is afraid of all animals that he runs home when he sees an animal on the street and he won't go to the zoo or circus. I feel that he is missing out on a lot of fun because of this fear.

A NY CHILD who is afraid of animals misses a lot because tame animals like dogs and cats can give a child real companionship. It is understandable, however, that your son is afraid of animals after the terrifying experience he had when he was younger.

Now that he is getting old enough to reason with, you should be able to point out to him that some animals are tame while others are not, that some animals are good playmates while others are not, and that how an animal treats a person often depends on how the person treats the animal. As your son grows older, I am sure he will lose some of the fear of animals he now has, although it is likely that he will never completely recover from his early experience and be a real animal-lover.

Fear of water

My husband claims that the best way to teach a child to swim is to throw him into deep water and let him swim. I argue that this will terrify a child so he will never want to learn to swim. Who is right?

Y OU ARE far more likely to be right about this matter than your husband. Swimming is not an inherited trait, like walking. It must be learned. Throwing a child who cannot swim into deep water will not only *not* teach him to swim but it will also terrify him to the point where he stiffens up and this will make swimming impossible. It is far better to wait until a child *asks* to learn to swim than to try to force him into swimming before he is ready. Let your child play safely at the shore of the lake or ocean and let him build up a real liking for water. Later, when his friends start to swim and he shows a desire to learn, that will be time enough to teach him to swim.

chapter 14

Promoting good
work habits

WE Americans rate *efficiency* very high. The slow ones may have just as much ability, but they fall by the wayside, outdistanced by the more efficient ones. Long before their childhood years are over, the laggards realize they spend more time on a given task than their friends. They see their achievements drop below those of their friends, and they are unhappy about their slowness.

Children need good work habits

GOOD work habits—an essential basis of efficiency—don't just happen or develop over night. And just *wanting* to be efficient isn't enough. *To acquire good work habits, a person must have the know-how as well as the desire and willingness to spend time and effort.*

Left to their own devices, children can and sometimes do develop good work habits. But most children, without guidance or help along this line, develop into dawdlers who work far

95

below their capacities, and spend more energy but accomplish far less than they are really capable of doing. Even when they do develop good work habits through trial and error, it is often after childhood is over and the precious years of their schooling are a thing of the past.

Good work habits are essential to good adjustment in the home, in school, and in all relationships with friends. That's why the sooner a child learns to do things the right way, the easy and quick way, the satisfying and profitable way, the better off he will be.

Suggestions to follow

H ERE are four suggestions that will help you promote good work habits in your child:

1. *When you assign a child a task, show him, at the same time, how to do it.* This is important not only when the task is a new one, but also when he has done it before. In this way, you can see for yourself if he has slipped back into inefficient methods. If he has, you can help him to correct any inefficiencies in the way he goes about the task before it is too late. This is just as important if he is building a castle out of sand, cleaning up his room, or doing his homework. Good habits in play carry over to work and thus increase his efficiency in whatever he does.

2. *Encourage your child to study the job he is doing to see if he can figure out for himself any short-cuts or energy-savers.* You cannot hope to follow him around and check up on his work habits all his life. You can, however, show him how to develop habits of efficiency so he can work out his own methods of doing things. Making him efficiency-minded from the start is a good way of transferring the responsibility of forming good work habits from your shoulders to his.

3. *Make working efficiently a game in which the child competes with himself to improve his work methods.* Children are always ready for a game. Nothing is more satisfying to them than to see themselves beating their own records. Even with young children you can introduce competition with their previous work by using a clock to show them where the hands were yesterday when they finished supper as compared with where the hands are today. A chart on which you record their improvements in the form of a star will give them an

added desire to work harder to improve their past records.

The timing habit will not take the joy out of living, as many parents believe; the child does not regard it as being "pushed" but rather as a game. Watching the hands of a clock is not irritating to a child as it may be to an adult; it adds spice to the activity.

Timing adds spice

4. *Give your child a motive to develop good work habits.* This should take the form of a personal reward, not an obligation imposed on him by you. Let him see for himself how much extra time it gives him to play or do what he wants to do. Be sure to praise him for his improvements so that he will feel that it has been well worth while.

Dawdling

My son, who is just 4 years old, dawdles over his meals until his food is completely cold. Then he doesn't want to eat it. Should I heat up the food, or what?

Cold food is likely to be tasteless to a child just as it is to an adult. It should encourage your son to eat his meal if you heated up the food when it became cold. More important, try to find out why he is dawdling. Is it because he does not like the food or because feeding himself a complete meal is a tiring task for him and he needs help? You can quickly find the answers to these questions by watching your son.

If the dawdling occurs only occasionally, you will know that the food he has been given at the meal is not one of his favorites; otherwise he would eat it more quickly, even if he were tired. If the dawdling occurs only at the end of a meal, it suggests that he is getting tired and needs some help in the feeding. Offer to do this and, if he accepts, you will know you are on the right track. The important thing is to get to the root of the dawdling before it settles into a habit.

How much instruction?

How much should a parent show a child about the best ways to do things? Won't this stifle the child's initiative?

A young child is an inexperienced child. As a result, it is difficult if not impossible for him to work out methods of doing things for himself. Therefore, he must have help. Each year, as he grows older and more experienced, he should be able to take over more and more responsibility. Never, under any conditions, try to force your way of doing things on a child. This is what makes him resentful and kills his initiative. Instead, show him how you do things and ask him if he has any suggestions for improvements. This will stimulate his imagination and keep his initiative alive. At the same time, it will give him direction in place of the blind trial-and-error he would be forced to use if he had no help or guidance from you.

Clumsy actions

My son, who is 7 years old, does everything in a clumsy, awkward way. Will he get over this as he grows older?

DOING things in a clumsy fashion usually means that the child has not had enough guidance in learning to do them in a more efficient manner. If you don't give your child this help, there is still a chance that he will be less clumsy in time, as he works out more efficient methods of doing things either by a thoughtful study of his methods or by imitating someone who is more efficient than he. You could, however, do a lot to speed up this improvement by pointing out to him where he could make improvements and by showing him short-cuts or less clumsy methods of action. If there is no evidence of poor muscular coordination due to a physical cause, then there is no need for a child of your son's age to do things in a clumsy manner. The trouble can be traced to poor work habits.

Study and radio or records

My children are all in school, ranging from third grade to senior high school. The older children insist they can study better if they are listening to the radio or records while they are studying. So, of course, the young ones feel that they should do the same. Can children study well when they are listening to music?

EXPERIMENTS have shown time and again that a person cannot do two things at the same time unless one is so automatic, through constant practice, that no attention need be given to it. A skilled knitter, for example, may knit while reading and read just as quickly and with as much understanding as a person who does not knit. But, if the knitter must count stitches in putting in a design, her attention must shift from her reading to her knitting.

Studying cannot be done automatically nor can listening to music. So the child shifts from listening to his program to studying his lesson, and then back to the radio. Naturally he gets little benefit from his studying and little pleasure from his records or radio listening. It would be far better and more satisfying to study hard, finish, then give undivided attention to the music.

Older children, who have learned to write and spell fairly automatically, may be able to copy some of their work, such as a composition, while listening to music, but the finished product is usually full of errors. A younger child, who has not yet learned to spell or write as automatically, cannot do anything but a bad job if he attempts to copy or study while listening to music.

Don't let your children's arguments fool you. Most children try to convince their parents that they become better students if they are permitted to listen to records or the radio while studying. Their grades do not justify this argument. They spend much more time on their studies than they should and, from the long view, they are developing habits of divided attention which make concentration difficult if not impossible.

Working in pairs

Is it wise to encourage children to work in pairs
or do they do better when they work alone?

Fᴏʀ any work that does not require close concentration, such as routine household tasks, making things in their play, or playing a team game, children do better in pairs than alone. By working with someone, they have a pace-setter who keeps them from dawdling. They are also inspired to do their best to be able to compete with their teammate. Even more important, it is fun to do things with others, no matter how much hard work it takes. However, when the task requires close concentration, as in the case of studying a school lesson, working in pairs is likely to be distracting. In such cases, children are likely to dawdle and to develop habits of working below the level of their abilities.

Study position

I maintain that a person cannot study well if lying down,
but my son says he can. Who is right?

Yᴏᴜ are right and your son is wrong about this matter. Lying down to study is very bad for the eyes, especially during childhood when the eye muscles are still weak. It also encourages the child to relax his body and with this comes a loss of his concentration. As a result, he grows sleepy, his mind wanders, and he does very poor· work, taking far more time for the work than its quality or quantity would justify. Insist that your son sit up when he studies. Give him a straight-back chair suited to his height so that he will not cramp any muscles by sitting on a chair not suited to his size, and see to it that he has a properly placed light so there will be no eyestrain from reading. Good work habits depend on the kind of work environment the person has just as much as on his methods of work.

Resistance to suggestions

Whenever I suggest that my 10-year-old daughter do something a different way—and I only make such suggestions when I see she is doing the thing in a clumsy, awkward way—she becomes annoyed and persists in doing it her own way. Am I wrong in interfering?

TRYING to help your daughter to improve her work habits is not really "interfering," even though she may interpret it as such. Since she has taken this stubborn, resisting attitude toward your suggestions, the best thing to do under the circumstances is to let her go ahead in her own way. She may ask you for help if you do not suggest helping her, and she may even work out better methods for herself. If you sit back and do nothing, you will, at least, have the satisfaction of knowing that you have not antagonized her and driven her into persisting in doing the things the inefficient way. It may be a consolation to you to know that many boys and girls of your daughter's age behave just as she does, and that they call loudest for help when they get in deep water and do not know how to get out.

Handling slowness

When my 5-year-old daughter is poking over something I ask her to do, I usually take over the task and do it myself. My husband says I shouldn't do this as it encourages the child to be slow so as to get out of doing things she doesn't want to do. Is he right?

YOUR husband is about 99 per cent correct. Occasionally a child does not have a hidden motive for poking, but most children learn quickly that by poking they can get out of doing things they do not want to do. I am quite sure your daughter has learned this little trick or else your husband would not have said what he did. Instead of taking over the task as you have been doing, show the child how to do it more quickly and then give her an incentive to speed up. You can say, for example, "After you have finished emptying all the scrap baskets, I have an interesting new picture book I want to show you." I am sure you will see a marked increase in speed and fewer complaints about doing a job she may not enjoy.

Speed and nervousness

Won't it make children nervous if parents expect them to do things too quickly?

EXPECTING anyone to work beyond his "congenial pace," or the speed with which he can do things comfortably but not so comfortably that he will dawdle, certainly does give rise to nervous tension. This is not only fatiguing but it usually causes the person to make lots of mistakes. Never push a child beyond the speed he can use comfortably. You can quickly tell if you are doing this by whether the child seems rushed and confused, and if he starts to make careless mistakes. If he does, let him slow down to a pace he can handle comfortably and efficiently. Parents should expect children to do things only at their own speed, not at the parents' speed. Naturally a child who is not as experienced or as strong as an adult cannot hope to keep up to the pace set by an adult.

Studying with child

I often study with my children in the sense that I have them read their lessons out loud to me, I hear their spelling, or I watch them while they are doing their arithmetic problems. Will this make them so dependent upon me that they will not be able to do their lessons alone?

IF YOU are merely helping your children to establish good work habits, they will be able to stand on their own feet and will not need your help, once their study habits are established. If, on the other hand, you do so much for them that they come to rely upon you, you will make them dependent to the point where they will not be able to cope with their school lessons alone. They will feel so insecure if something keeps you from helping them that they will not do their lessons, they will become emotionally upset, or they will do their lessons so slowly and badly that they will fail.

Try coming in and out when your children are studying. Sample the different lessons as they study them but don't stay with them the whole time. You might, for example, watch over the child's shoulder while he starts a problem. Then, if you see he is on the right track, leave him alone and let him finish the lesson by himself. Hear the child read a few lines and if he is reading well, tell him to finish by himself. This will enable you to check up on your children's study habits without, at the same time, creating in them a feeling of dependency on you.

Working with two hands

I have been told that children should learn to do things equally well with both hands so they can do them faster and shift from one hand to another when they get tired. Is this a new theory and is it a good one?

TRAINING both hands is not exactly a new theory because it has been practiced for many years by some people. If your child is willing to practice doing such things as writing, throwing balls, painting, crayoning, cutting, or digging in the earth with first one hand then the other, he will find that he can do these things equally with both. Then encourage him, whenever conditions permit, to use both hands together. It will speed up what he is doing and it will be good training in muscle coordination to have his hands working in pairs instead of singly.

Mind-wandering

Whenever my child sits down to read or study, I notice he is looking off into space. His teacher tells me he does the same in class and often doesn't hear her question. How can I help him to concentrate on what he is doing?

THE best and only real cure for mind-wandering is development of interest. When a person's mind wanders off from the subject at hand, it is because he is bored with the subject. He begins to think of something more interesting and, before he realizes what is happening, he is completely wrapped up in his thoughts. You can help your child to concentrate only if you can help him to see the interesting aspects of the things he finds boring. One very good way to bring interest into an otherwise boring subject is to try to make it seem *personal* to the child. If, for example, he can think of pennies when he does the arithmetic problems, the figures of arithmetic will not seem so meaningless to him. Similarly, if he can imagine himself living in the days of early America, his American history will become more alive and more interesting.

Paper and pencil habit

Is it true that a person can study better if he uses paper and pencil to take notes and should I encourage my children to develop this habit?

THE paper and pencil habit is a splendid check on mind-wandering. When a person has a pencil in hand, ready to use it, he is more likely to keep his mind on the subject in preparation for use of the pencil than if he is merely reading. Suggest to your children that they make occasional use of their pencils and paper so that they will see some point in having them. Tell them to underline a word they are unfamiliar with or to write it down on their papers. Suggest, also, that they be prepared to write down a few words after they finish reading or studying as a means of reminding them of what they have just read. As they grow older, they will thank you for teaching them good work methods when they were still young and before they developed bad habits that they must later break in order to do good work in or out of school.

chapter 15

Developing children's interests and talents

E VERY child has special interests and talents along some line, whether musical, athletic, or other. Perhaps his talent may not be great enough to class him a "genius"—but it serves as the basis of interests and activities which will bring him happiness and success in life. As a result, they are well worth the time and effort you give to their cultivation.

How to recognize talents

H ow can you know what talent or talents your child has and at what age can you recognize them? A talent shows itself in activities that are related to that talent. A child with musical ability, for example, will show an absorbing interest in listening to music. He will also take advantage of every possible opportunity to produce music of his own, either by playing with toy horns and drums, or by playing with any musical instrument in his home and making music of his own whenever he is permitted to touch these instruments.

By observing your child's behavior, therefore, you can tell what his interests and abilities are. The stronger the talent, the stronger his interest, and the more things he will do that are related to this interest.

A child needs opportunity

No one knows at what age a talent will show up, because that depends to a certain extent upon the environment of the child. Only when the right kind of environment is present can a talent be fostered. For instance: a child with mathematical ability may not show the first sign of this ability until he goes to school and has his first real contact with numbers. Similarly, a girl who, as a little child, is given no opportunity to do things in the kitchen for fear that she will hurt herself, may give no indication of her talent for cooking until she is old enough to have free access to the kitchen.

Encourage interest and ability

INTEREST and ability go hand in hand. That is why a wise parent will not only make every possible effort to learn what a child's talents are but will also give him the opportunities and encouragement necessary to develop these capacities to their peak. Only in this way can a child achieve real happiness and success. If you try to curb an interest or to turn the talent into channels foreign to it, the child will be unhappy. He will have little interest in the things his parents try to force him to do.

Talents need to be encouraged

Developing interests is easier than developing talents. Exposing a child to situations that encourage the development of his interests and helping him to appreciate the meaning of these situations generally does the trick. Interest development is really a salesmanship job. You must make the child feel that the interest comes from within *him,* not from your pressures, if you want to keep that interest alive.

You can't force an interest on a child

No matter how anxious you may be to have your child interested in good music and literature, for example, you will never win your goal by force. Make his contacts with these forms of art *pleasant.* That will bring you much closer to your goal. The more pleasant his contacts, the stronger his interests will become. That is why it is important to manage the child's environment in such a manner that he will not develop interests that may prove to be more harmful than helpful to him as he grows older.

No talent

My son, who is finishing third grade, seems to have no real interest in any of his school work. Does this mean that he has no talents at all?

Your son's talents may be of a non-scholarly kind. He may have a keen interest in shop work, in painting or drawing, in music, or in sports, but his school may not pay much attention to any of these activities. On the other hand, he may develop an interest in some school subject as he grows older and thus reveal a real ability in it. At present, his schooling is merely laying the foundations for his later studies. And, like all foundations, these are not always interesting to a child.

Don't jump to any conclusions about your child's interests or abilities at this time. Wait until he has been in school longer and has an opportunity to get enough background in different subjects to see where his interests and abilities lie. Perhaps not until he reaches junior high school will you find a strong interest along one line of studies.

Vocational tests

What can a child learn from vocational tests and at what age should they be given?

Vocational tests fall into two groups: the vocational *interest* tests and the vocational *aptitude* tests. The interest tests are given to help the child see where his interests lie; the aptitude tests measure his ability in different lines of work.

The real value of a vocational *interest* test is that it helps the child and the school counselor to see what types of activities hold the greatest interest for the child and thus enables him to know what schooling he needs in order to develop these interests. As a rule, children show pretty definite, clear-cut evidence of greater interest in one kind of work than in another. The usual age for giving vocational interest tests is during the second year of high school. The reason for this is that many high schools today offer boys and girls a variety of courses from which they are permitted to select those most closely related to the type of work they are planning to do when their schooling is completed. A boy who, for example, wants to go into some kind of professional work must select courses to prepare him for college. A girl who wants to enter business as soon as her high school course is completed is advised to take the secretarial rather than the college preparatory course.

Vocational *aptitude* tests are more often given in the senior or even junior year of high school than during the sophomore year. They are also given (as is true of vocational interest tests) during the college years. For the most part, these tests are of greater value for what they show the person he *cannot do* or is *not interested* in doing than for their direct guidance. After taking a vocational interest test, for example, boys and girls are pretty sure that they do not want to do this or that type of work because they have little or no interest in it. Even the best of the vocational aptitude tests are only rough measures of the person's true abilities in different lines of work.

Music tests

I would like to have my 7-year-old daughter taught to play the piano but I am not sure if she has enough musical talent to justify the time and money spent on music lessons. Is there any way of testing her musical talent before we decide about giving her music lessons?

THERE are several good musical aptitude tests. Many music teachers use them to determine whether the potential music students are gifted enough to justify their taking lessons. These tests do not tell how great a child's musical talent is. Their value lies in the fact that they pick out, with a high degree of accuracy, the child whose musical ability is so slight that even the best music lessons and the most conscientious work on the child's part would never make him a real musician. With this knowledge to guide them, parents must then decide whether they want to spend the money for lessons, and whether it is fair to their children to expect them to fight an uphill battle when they know the cards are heavily stacked against them from the very first.

Musical ability

Is it true that musical ability cannot be developed by good training?

BECAUSE musical ability is inborn, you cannot make a musician out of a person just by giving him good training. Even the best training available and the strongest possible desire on the child's part as well as on the part of his parents will not be enough to make a musician out of a child who lacks the necessary talent. If good training and parental ambition were enough to develop musical talent, the country would have many more musicians than it has!

It's too bad that many people believe that musical training and a desire to learn to perform musically will develop musical talent. It's too bad because far too often parents feel that their children are not taking full advantage of the musical opportunities offered them and, by blaming the children for this, parents stifle the children's interest in music.

This situation is not limited to music. The belief that a child can do whatever he wants to do in a given field of endeavor, provided he is given the training necessary, leads to many cases of feelings of inferiority in children. And it leads to resentment on the parents' part because their children have not shown adequate appreciation for their "advantages" or made proper use of them.

Talent not enough

My daughter has won several prizes in art contests. Her teachers tell me she has a career ahead if she will work at it. But she says she can only work when she is in the right mood. Is this true?

Your daughter is fortunate in having so much talent, but she will find out that talent alone is not enough. No artist can afford to wait for the right mood or inspiration, if she wants to make a successful career of her art. Success in any field depends on hard work and self-discipline as well as talent. Tell her to try beginning a drawing or painting, and she will find that the mood and inspiration will come. She will find, too, that the more she works, the more her art will improve and the more her talent will grow.

Curbing talents

My husband feels that musicians are "sissies." He wants our son, who is talented in music and very serious about it, to go into business. He even ridicules our boy's interest in hearing classical music and teases him about his "sissy" music lessons. Can my husband's actions discourage our son and curb his talent?

Your husband's tactics may discourage your son by giving him a feeling of inferiority about his musical interests and, even worse, about his ability to make a success in the musical world. It is unfair and unkind of your husband to label your son's musical interest and talent as "sissy." Some of our greatest musicians and composers have been men and they have not been "sissies." Their interests did, to some extent, make them different from the hard-headed business men, but they were not "sissies" in the sense that most people think of "sissies."

No matter what your husband says or does, he cannot kill your son's musical talent, but he can certainly produce such unfavorable attitudes in your son that the boy will not make the most of his talent. This would be most unfortunate because it would mean years of unhappiness and regret for your boy. Furthermore, if the boy's interest *is* definitely in music, he will never make a really good business man unless the business is closely related to the field of music, as in the case of a music shop. As a result, he will be both unhappy and unsuccessful—far from what any parent wants of his son.

Talent and career

My daughter, who is just 9 years old, loves to dance. However, I wonder if it is worth the time and money for tap lessons. I doubt if she is good enough to make a living from dancing. Wouldn't it be better for her to spend the time on studies that she can use later?

I F YOU are thinking of dancing lessons solely as a preparation for a career, I can understand why you question their worth. Few children have the talent needed for this. But dancing lessons can still be a valuable part of your child's education—especially since she loves dancing. They can help her develop grace, poise, and self-confidence and these will be assets all through her life, no matter what career she chooses. They can also help her develop work habits—through her practicing—that will enable her to study her other lessons more effectively. And she may learn to dance well enough to appear on school programs and entertain her friends, and this can also help build her self-confidence and give her much happiness.

Writing talent

My son has a very vivid imagination for a 7-year-old and likes to tell his friends stories. I have written down some of them and am thinking of sending them to a publisher. Does this indicate that he has talent for writing and should we encourage him to be a writer?

B Y ALL means encourage your son to develop his storytelling ability and to study hard on his composition in school. His school training in this field, as he grows older, will be a great help to him in improving his style of writing. In the meantime, encourage him to tell stories and, as soon as he learns to read, encourage extensive reading of good literature. But don't set your heart on the child's becoming a writer. He may not have a strong enough ability in this line to compete successfully with other writers. However, in whatever line of work he eventually enters, he will find writing a great asset. Moreover, writing and reading will always be a source of interest and inspiration to him.

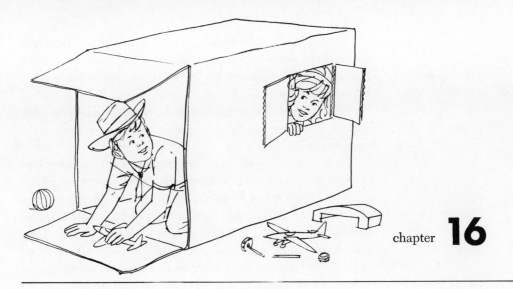

chapter 16

Making the most
of play

PLAY is the child's chief occupation. And it is through his play that he develops physically, mentally, and morally. Not only do his muscles harden and become coordinated from his play but his general well-being is improved. He eats and sleeps better, he is happier, and he has fewer emotional outbursts *after* playing than before. Too much play, on the other hand, can fatigue a child to such a point where the good effects of play will be lost and his fretfulness will make him a difficult child to manage.

Other values

PLAY stimulates a child's imagination, improves his memory, and offers him opportunities for reasoning. It makes him mentally alert and this, in turn, helps him to make good adjustments to life by preparing him to meet any problems life may present. Often a child learns more from his play about how to meet practical situations of an everyday sort than he learns from his schooling.

Getting along with people is a necessity if one is to live in a civilized world. There is no place where a child can learn this better than through his play. His contacts with other children in school and Sunday school are so limited and so regulated by rules that he has little time to associate with children in a give-and-take manner. This type of association he must get from his play.

Character-building, likewise, cannot occur in school as it can on the playground. So long as there is a parent or teacher to tell the child what to do and what not to do, he will not learn to stand on his own feet and make his own decisions. This he must learn in his *free play* with those his age. *They* will let him know what they like and dislike in others. If he wants to be popular and have fun with other children, he must learn to submerge his interests into those of the group and behave as his playmates expect of him.

Play means suitable equipment

BECAUSE play is so important a factor in a child's life, *how* he plays should not be left to chance. The equipment given him to stimulate his play should be *selected,* not assembled in a haphazard manner. These materials are so important in the child's whole pattern of development that their planning is worth unlimited time and thought. They are also worth personal sacrifices of time on the parent's part to direct and teach the child so that he will play in the most beneficial manner.

How a child will play will depend partly on the equipment he has available and partly on how he learns to use this equipment. Just giving him the equipment is not enough. He may, through trial and error, hit upon ways to use this equipment that will give him pleasure. But he will have more pleasure and certainly more benefit if he is given some *direction* in how to use his play equipment.

Children aren't alike in their needs and interests, but there are certain types of play equipment that *every* child needs and enjoys. In planning the equipment for your child's play, be sure to supply him with materials to stimulate *different* forms of play. Don't make the mistake of overloading him with too much equipment of one type and too little or none of another type.

Equipment for exploratory play

THIS should include simple baby toys such as rattles, blocks, spools on strings, Plakies, cradle gyms, and soft, cuddly dolls and animals. This should be available to him between his second and third months. By the time he is ready to walk, he will want to explore everything in his environment. Turn over to him some old pots and pans, kitchen spoons, especially the large wooden type, metal measuring cups, magazines and newspapers to tear, and be sure he has water toys for his bath. For summer, have a wading pool in the back yard and water toys to float in it.

Before the first birthday

Equipment to develop the large muscles

ON HIS first birthday, and each year from then until he is ready to play games and sports, add to the supply of equipment that will be used for strenuous outdoor play. This should include push and pull toys, tricycles (later, bicycles), roller skates, ice skates, water wings for water play, jungle gym, slides, swings, sleds, and large balls.

Toys for out of doors

As soon as your child is walking with good balance and control, he will be ready for this equipment. At first, his use will be largely exploratory. He will, for example, wheel his tricycle around for days before he attempts to ride it, and he will push his roller skates around on the floor as if they were trains before putting them on his feet. But, if the equipment is available and he is shown how to use it, it will not be long before it becomes a part of his daily play.

Equipment for constructive play

EVERY child enjoys making things just for the fun of doing so. He is not critical of the finished product, though he enjoys having someone praise it and likes to compare his achievements with those of his playmates. Making things is a good form of play for rainy days and for times when the child is ill or tired. It also helps to develop the smaller muscles of the hands which are not given adequate exercise in out-of-door games. For these reasons, every child should not only have materials for making things but he should be shown how to

Things to make and do

111

use them. This type of equipment needs more demonstration, if it is to be used pleasurably, than do most other forms.

For the 2- and 3-year-old, sand and sand toys, soap bubble pipes, large crayons, paints and paint brushes, clay, and blocks are good for constructions. After 3, the child is ready to cut and paste, to weave, model with clay, saw and hammer, help with the mixing and baking of cookies, and knit. The skills learned in childhood play are useful not only as foundations for muscle skills but also as a means of developing favorable attitudes toward work of a similar nature as he grows older.

Suitable materials

Equipment for dramatization

Every child from the time he is 3 or 4 years of age until he goes to school, enjoys imagining that he is someone else doing something he has heard about in stories or has seen in pictures. So it is important to provide him with the materials he needs to dress up and to construct scenery for his play. This, of course, does not mean that he needs regular costumes or stage settings. A few cast off pieces of clothing, some old pieces of furniture, draperies, bed spreads, or dishes that have been cracked and chipped are all he needs for his dramatizations. His active imagination will do the rest and he will have no need for expensive equipment for this form of play.

Simple material for acting

Equipment for games

The games most children in America like are the running games and ball games. By the time they are 8 or 9 years old, they will want to learn to play the games the big boys or girls play. At first, all they need are balls of different sizes. Later, they will need baseball gloves and bats, tennis rackets, basketballs and baskets, and footballs. But more important than the equipment is the know-how. The child must be shown how to throw and catch balls and, later, how to use his tennis rackets, basketballs, footballs, or hockey sticks.

Running games and ball games

Equipment for amusements

There are many times when a child enjoys being amused. He likes to hear stories, to be read to, to listen to the radio, and to records, and to watch television. It is never too early to start his own library by buying some of the inexpensive books that are now available. If possible, buy an inexpensive nursery record player, too, and a selection of records. Choose books and records carefully, keeping in mind his age and comprehension level. Ask your librarian to help you. And take him to the library, too, for the story-telling hour! Check the television programs, too, for ones suitable for him and which he will enjoy.

Stories and music for enjoyment

Playtime

I feel that children should have as much time as possible to play. My husband thinks they should do some work and not play all the time. Who is right?

Your husband has the right idea about a combination of work and play rather than either alone. While "all work and no play will make Jack a dull boy," so will all play make him dull because he will become bored and indifferent toward his play opportunities. To get the maximum enjoyment from their play, children need some duties and responsibilities to balance the day.

How much of their time will be given over to duties will, of course, depend upon the children's ages. You can tell if you are hitting a happy balance by the child's attitude and behavior. If he seems happy and content with both his duties and his play, you know the balance is right for him. If, on the other hand, he shows boredom with either his work or his play, it means that proportionally too much time is devoted to it.

Supervision of play

How much should a parent supervise her children's play? When I was young, parents used to give their children toys and turn them loose in the back yard or in the playroom. Now one hears that parents should supervise a child's play.

It is true that children, in past generations, were turned loose to play as they wished. Many children enjoyed this and profited by the freedom to use their own initiative. Other children enjoyed themselves but got little benefit from the time they spent in play. The present-day emphasis on supervised play is to keep children from being hurt—life is certainly more filled with hazards than it used to be—and to show children how to make the best use of their play equipment so they can get the most enjoyment and benefit from it. Toys and all types of play equipment are so much more complicated today than they used to be that a child really needs some help in learning to use them.

Making things

My son Johnny, who is just 5 years old, doesn't seem to like to play with his toys. All he wants to do is make things with saws and hammers, clay, or paints. Isn't it better for a child his age to be playing with his toys?

Your son *is playing* even if he isn't using toys. What is play for one person may be work for another. You may not think it fun to make things but your son obviously does. Otherwise, he would not choose the hammer, saw, and paint brush in preference to the toys you have given him.

Let him play as he wishes. If you try to force him to play with his toys instead of making things, you will find that he will get little fun from what he is doing and complain constantly because he has "nothing to do." Your son must have some constructive talent, otherwise he would not want to spend his play time making things. Encourage this and spend the money you would spend on toys for equipment to make things with. By doing this, you will enable your son to play as he wishes and in a manner that gives him greatest enjoyment.

Dangerous toys

What toys are dangerous for children, and how can a parent know what to buy?

Today, manufacturers of children's toys are doing all they can to make their toys as safe as possible. Not all imported toys nor all toys of cheap construction, however, are as safe as they should be. Therefore, it is wise to examine a toy very carefully before permitting a child to have it. If the child is playing with another child's toys, examine them, too. In general, the danger spots to look for are eyes of stuffed animals or dolls that can be pulled out; paint that chips off; celluloid that cracks and develops sharp edges; metal or wood toys put together in such a way that small pieces can be pulled off; pistols that shoot water or marbles; and tricycles or roller skates that can lose a wheel and thus throw a child.

It is a good policy to check a child's toys every day or two to make sure they are in good condition. This is especially important with baby toys or toys for a toddler because very young children like to put things in their mouths more than older children do.

Movies

*How soon should children be permitted to go to movies,
and how often should they go?*

IT IS best to keep children away from moving picture theatres as long as possible, because looking at a moving picture is somewhat of an eyestrain, even for adults whose eyes are stronger than children's. If you have a projector, why not rent some children's films for special occasions, such as birthdays, children's parties, and holidays, and have moving picture shows at home? You can control the time your child sees a picture at home better than when he goes to a movie theatre. If possible, keep him away from moving picture theatres until he is 5 or 6 years old.

Record-player for children

*My children, 3, 5, and 8 years of age, all like to listen to music.
I have been thinking of getting a record-player for them, but
I am afraid they are too young to handle such an instrument
and that they will break it or the records.
What is your opinion?*

IT WOULD be foolish to put money into an expensive record-player for children to use. There are, however, many inexpensive "nursery" models on the market which are made for children's use. If you show your two older children how to play records on this type of player, they can get much pleasure and enjoyment from it. These models are easy for children to operate and the records are made of non-breakable plastic so there is little danger that your children will damage or destroy them. In giving your children an opportunity to listen to records, you will be fostering a love of music that can give them many happy hours.

Television

*How much eyestrain comes from watching television and what
types of programs should a 5-year-old be permitted to watch?*

EVEN the best TV sets today may have quite a lot of flicker. This causes eyestrain. You can cut down on some of the harmful effects to your child's eyes by insisting that he sit a reasonable distance away from the set to avoid the bad effects of flicker and that he watch for no more than 15 minutes at a time.

As for suitable programs, that will depend upon what your station has to offer. Check the program before you permit him to see it. If it is a serial, you can tell from watching one or two programs what sort it is and if there is much in it that can be terrifying to a child. Generally the morning and early afternoon programs are more suitable for children. You will be wise to check very carefully any late afternoon or evening program your child watches.

Cheap toys

I find my children are so destructive with toys that I hesitate to put money into good toys. Won't cheap toys answer their needs as well as expensive ones?

No, I don't think so. If your children are destructive with their toys, I think you would find cheap toys so flimsily made that they would not be worth the money you put into them. Instead of buying cheap toys, why not train your children to take better care of good toys? They are made to stand a reasonable amount of wear-and-tear, and they are far less likely to go to pieces when played with than are the cheap toys. Furthermore, they are less dangerous because they do not splinter as much or have sharp edges, as do the less expensive types of toys.

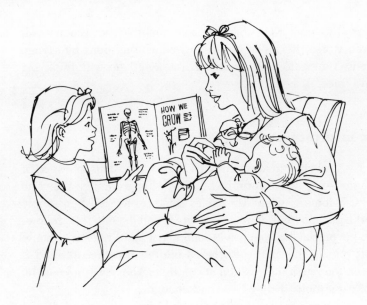

chapter 17

Sex education

Wнат your child learns about sex is not nearly so important as *how* he learns it. If he gets faulty information from outsiders, whether playmates or adults, this may distort his attitude toward anything relating to sex. And this may leave a lasting impression that will color his whole behavior toward members of the opposite sex and lay the foundation for an unhappy marriage.

Attitude is important

In childhood, information about sex is far less important than the child's *attitude* toward sex. To say this another way: the child can be harmed far more when greater sex knowledge is combined with fear, shame, or disgust, than when limited sex information is combined with a wholesome, healthy attitude.

The kind of attitude your child develops will depend largely upon *you*. If *you* are shy, embarrassed, and self-conscious when you answer your child's questions, he will

117

naturally think the subject is something to be ashamed of. Even worse: if you refuse to answer his questions by saying, "It isn't nice to talk about such things," he will think sex isn't "nice."

How to give sex information

I T IS far better to answer the child's sex questions in a specific manner—not in the form of a lecture. For example: When he asks, "Mommy, where do babies come from?" tell him simply and truthfully, but don't go into great detail. Only if he follows up his original question with another related question should *Questions* you pursue the matter further. Children become confused if *don't call* given too much information at one time. They let you know by *for lectures* their questions if they have had enough.

Be sure you use words your child can understand. If you need to use technical terms, explain what they mean. To make sure he understands, show him either in a picture or on his own body what organ you are talking about and where it is.

The child By the time your child is 5 or 6 years old, it is wise to read *of 5 or 6* to him simple explanations of the origin of babies, why boys and girls, men and women, are different, and how a baby grows in the mother's body. Read these stories to him just as you would read any other stories. Show him the pictures in the book and help him to understand them in relation to his own body.

What "growing Shortly after a child enters school, during his first grade, *up" means* begin to acquaint him with the fact that it will not be long now before he begins to "grow up." Gradually, each year, explain to him what "growing up" means: the changes in height, weight, and body proportions to those of men and women; the development of the secondary sex characteristics, such as hair on the body and change of voice; and the changes that take place in the sex organs themselves.

The meaning By the time they are 9 or 10 years old, both boys and girls *of puberty* should be thoroughly familiar with the meaning of menstrua-
changes tion and nocturnal emissions. Children today often begin their puberty changes when they are 10 or 11 years old. Knowing several years ahead of time what will happen to them will go a long way toward quieting any fears or dreads they may have regarding these changes.

Stork myth

*My mother maintains that children are too young to
understand the real origin of babies and that it is better to tell
them the stork brings babies. Is she right about this?*

YOUR mother is right about a young child's not being able to understand fully
the meaning of conception, prenatal growth, and birth. But it is not necessary for
children to understand all these facts *until they are old enough to understand
them.* On the other hand, if children are told that storks bring babies, they will
sooner or later discover from their playmates that this is not true. Then they will
wonder about other things their parents tell them, causing a serious loss of confidence in their parents. Play safe: tell your child the *correct* facts about the origin
of babies. The best way to do this is to answer his questions and not give him
information that is not related to his questions. When he is ready for more advanced information, he will let you know by the type of question he asks.

Seed in mother's body

*Someone told my 6-year-old son that babies come from
seeds in their mothers' bodies. Now Philip wants
to know how the seed got there. What should I tell him?*

TELL him the truth. You don't have to go into detail about the whole matter at
this age but, since he raised the question, it is best to answer it. Tell him that
fathers put the seeds in the mothers' bodies when they want to have babies. This
will probably satisfy him for now. If it doesn't, tell him the whole story or as much
as he seems to understand. If you don't tell him, you can be sure he will try to
get the answer from someone else—and it may not be the type of answer you
would like him to have.

Talking about sex

*My 7-year-old daughter, Cathy, comes home with all kinds of stories
and jokes about sex. She gets them from her classmates
in school. I tell her that nice children don't talk about such things,
but she says they all do. Isn't there some way to put
a stop to children's talking about sex?*

THE only way you can keep children from talking about sex is to let them grow
up in a shell, away from all living humans. This, I am sure, you would not consider

doing. Children, the nice as well as the not-so-nice, all talk about sex in some way at some time. You simply cannot stop them, because sex is important to them, just as to adults, but in a different way.

The smutty stories and dirty jokes that circulate in every school are not harmful to a child if he *already* has a good understanding of the meaning of sex. If, however, his *first* introduction to sex information comes from smutty stories and dirty jokes, it is most unfortunate. Under such conditions, the child's whole attitude toward sex is likely to become so warped that it may affect him unfavorably for the rest of his life.

Shocked parents

I told my children the facts of life before they entered first grade.
When classmates say wrong things about sex, my children set
them straight. Today, Marion, my 8-year-old, came home in tears:
her friend Judy's mother said Marion could no longer play with Judy because
Marion talked about sex. What can I do?

WHY not telephone or go see Judy's mother and tell her why Marion talked about sex to her child? She may not realize how much young children talk about sex when they get together and she may have made the mistake of not preparing her child for this. Naturally the mother would rather have the facts about sex come from *her* rather than from her child's classmates. It is a pity that she has taken this attitude toward your child but it is perfectly natural for Marion to join in the talk about sex and to set her little friend straight if she thinks she was confused or ignorant on the subject.

Just as a caution: you might do well to tell your children not to discuss sex too freely with their friends as sometimes parents misunderstand it. Tell them also to suggest to their friends that they go to their parents for information if they want to know anything. Emphasize that this is a parent's responsibility, and that you feel your children should not try to take over.

Nocturnal emissions

I feel that my husband should tell our son about the stains
on his pajamas and bed clothes. He maintains that
I should do this. What is your opinion?

MY OPINION is that the boy should get the information about nocturnal emissions right now and from a person who can tell him exactly what they mean so the boy will not get twisted ideas about them. If your husband is not willing to take over this responsibility, and since a boy is likely to be very embarrassed if he gets such information from a woman, I suggest that you send him to the doctor for a complete briefing about what is happening to him. Otherwise, the boy will become very concerned about the possible loss of his virility.

Masturbation

Is it true that masturbation is likely to lead to physical weakness and even to insanity?

WHILE it is true that masturbation is a socially unacceptable form of behavior, it does no damage except to cause marked feelings of guilt on the part of the person who engages in it. There is no medical evidence to show that it weakens a person or causes insanity. Very few adolescents, whether boys or girls, escape some masturbating. This usually lasts only a few years and then they stop it as their sex organs develop fully. If you suspect that your child is masturbating, ask the doctor to explain it to him and to suggest substitutes for relief of the tension that leads to masturbation.

Menstruation

My 10-year-old daughter is starting to grow very rapidly. Our doctor says he expects her to start to menstruate in another year or two. Is this the time to tell her about menstruation or should I wait until nearer the time? What shall I say?

ONCE a child, whether a boy or a girl, starts the "puberty growth spurt," you cannot predict when the moment of sexual maturity will come. For that reason, it is wise to prepare your daughter at once. Tell her about menstruation, what it means, and answer any questions she may ask. Be sure to stress the fact that it is a normal event and nothing to be frightened about or ashamed of. Don't under any conditions refer to it as "sickness." "Sickness" suggests that there is something wrong with her and creates the impression in her mind that she is not well at the time of her menstrual period.

Before menstruation begins, she should know that for a year or two her menstrual periods are likely to be very irregular and painful. She may have severe cramps, a bad backache, vomiting, dizziness, and many other unpleasant experiences. Tell her this is normal because the organs are just beginning to function and it takes time for them to get regulated.

Tell her also what she can and cannot do during her menstrual period. Today, doctors advise doing the things normally done instead of going to bed and keeping quiet. As a result of living a normal life, girls of today suffer much less during their menstrual periods than did girls of the past.

It would be well worth the price of an office visit to take your daughter to the doctor and have the doctor explain to her what she can and cannot do safely at the time of her menstruation. The doctor can also give her medicine should she suffer from cramps. As most girls are very self-conscious about this whole matter, it would be better to take her to a woman doctor than to a man.

Adult body

My 5-year-old daughter, Linda, came into my room one day when I was undressed. She asked me why she didn't have some of the features in her body that I had. I didn't know how to answer her. How can I set her straight about such matters and when is the best time to do it?

THE best time is when a child asks questions. As you neglected this opportunity, take advantage of the first possible moment to make up for it. Get a book that shows pictures of adults in the nude. Any book on sex education for children will have such pictures. Then explain to Linda the differences between male and female bodies not only in adulthood but in childhood as well. Tell her why these differences occur. And, most important of all, *don't be embarrassed about it*. A child takes such information in as matter-of-fact a manner as if you were talking about how bread is made or why a light switch turns on the electric fan. If you are embarrassed, she will be, too, and this will lead to very unfavorable attitudes on her part.

chapter 18

Good manners
can be learned

So MANY children today have poor manners! No wonder that Mary and Dick—if they have *good* manners—stand out from the crowd and win nods of approval from adults as well as from their companions.

At any age, there is nothing so attractive as good manners. This is especially true when the child draws nearer the teens. At this age, being liked by members of the opposite sex is just as important as being liked by one's own sex. And good manners go a long way toward winning that precious popularity.

The heart of good manners

ARE manners just polish—something on the outside? No, they are an expression of an *inner desire* "to do unto others as you would have them do unto you." Manners help a child to appreciate what others do for him. They make others *want* to keep on doing things for him. They are a necessary part in the social adjustment of a child, no matter what his age.

But a child doesn't inherit his manners. He must *learn* them, just as he learns to speak, to write, and to do other things. And, like the rest of what he learns, he can't learn good manners overnight. They must come gradually, as the need for them arises. He must also have a *desire* to do things that will please others and to show his appreciation of what they do for him.

How manners are learned

This is very important, too: he must be in surroundings where good manners are usual, not rare. Does the child live in a home where no doors are banged, no voices raised in anger, and no one takes things for granted or makes unreasonable demands? Then he, too, will absorb and imitate what goes on around him. But is he always hearing Daddy interrupt others or Mommy saying "Do this" without bothering to add "please"? Then you can't expect *him* to do otherwise.

How can good manners be taught?

FIRST: *Set a good example in the home*. This is basic to the teaching of good manners. This means that parents must watch their own manners at all times. It does not mean taking a set of hard and fast rules from a book on etiquette. It does mean we must apply, in our daily living, the little kindnesses and courtesies that are the foundation stones of good manners. It means showing appreciation and understanding for all that others do or try to do for us, and for their motives, their opinions, their feelings, and their welfare.

Three rules for teaching manners

Second: *Provide daily practice*. There should be no such thing as "company manners." What is right for company should be right for the family! Daily practice in good manners speeds up the learning of good manners. And, even more important, practice makes good manners so habitual that the child does not feel self-conscious and ill-at-ease when he tries to do what he has been taught he should do when he is with other people.

And third: *Teach the child what to do and what to say at different times and with different people*. Rehearsing at home until the manners are learned is not only fun but it is also a good way to see that the child is learning the right thing. Suppose, for example, you are teaching him how to shake hands with people, how to hold a door so that an older person may pass ahead, or how to acknowledge a gift in speech or writing. Then practice this with your child until you are sure that he has mastered it.

124

But here is a word of caution. *Don't try to teach all the manners at one time.* Let your child master one form of good behavior before starting to learn another. Children learn quickly, especially when they have a good model to copy when they are at home. Wait until you are sure that one thing is well learned before you start teaching another. This avoids confusion in the child and eliminates any feeling he may have that you are expecting too much of him.

WHAT MANNERS SHOULD YOUNG CHILDREN LEARN?

B<small>Y THE</small> time a child reaches his tenth birthday, he should have mastered these rules of etiquette:

Manners related to other people

1. To say "How do you do?" and "Good-bye," looking straight at the person and smiling while saying these words.
2. To say, "Yes, Mrs. Jones," or "No, Mother," not just "yes" or "no."
3. To answer politely when spoken to by anyone, regardless of personal feelings toward that person.
4. To say "Pardon me," "Excuse me," or "I am sorry," when doing anything to interfere with what another is doing, such as walking in front or unintentionally interrupting when someone is speaking.
5. To give a seat in the room or bus to an older person.
6. To hold a door open for an older person to walk out first.

Helping your child get along with others

7. To pick up something another person has dropped and return it to that person.
8. To respect the privacy of others by not asking personal questions or by opening letters or boxes belonging to others, and by knocking and asking permission to enter another's room.
9. To ask permission to use things belonging to others and to return them in as good condition as they were when borrowed, or to offer to substitute a new article if the original was in any way damaged.
10. To cover the nose and mouth when coughing or sneezing, in order to avoid scattering germs that might give others colds.

11. To avoid all signs of amusement when others make mistakes and to offer to help them when they are in trouble.

12. To avoid ridiculing others or telling jokes which might hurt their feelings.

13. To respect the race, religion, manners, dress, and speech of others as he hopes and expects they will respect his.

14. To offer to do things for others when there is any indication that help would be welcomed, such as when they are carrying several bundles or when they are having difficulties in opening a door.

Manners related to visiting

1. To greet the hostess with a smile, a handshake, and the simple words, "How do you do?"

2. To be agreeable to any suggestions made by the host or hostess, and to be a good sport about whatever is suggested for activities.

3. To eat what refreshments are provided without refusals and to comment favorably on food liked.

4. To refrain from touching, examining, or playing with things belonging to the hostess or host unless permission is given.

5. To make no comments on what the hostess does, says, or has that might be interpreted as critical and might lead to hurt feelings.

*How to make
visits pleasant*

6. To offer to help with any work that is being done, such as the preparation of food, washing of dishes, or moving of furniture for play.

7. To put things back into place before leaving and to pick up any scraps or dirt that might have been brought in from play.

8. To thank the hostess graciously for a pleasant afternoon or party.

9. To write a brief but friendly "Thank you" note to the hostess after a party or to thank a child for a gift after a birthday party.

10. To be a gracious host or hostess when entertaining and to do all possible to see that the guests have a good time.

11. To be willing to do what guests want to do, even if contrary to his own wishes.

12. To plan entertainment and refreshments that will please his guests.

Learning how to be a good host or hostess

13. To help his parents prepare for guests and clean up after they leave.

14. To avoid any arguments or fights with guests and to refrain from doing or saying anything that might offend them or make them feel unwelcome.

15. To show no favoritism to any one guest when there are several present at the same time.

Table manners

1. Chewing food quietly and with the mouth closed.

2. Talking only when there is no food in the mouth.

3. Placing the napkin on the lap as soon as one is seated at the table, keeping it there until the meal is finished, then placing it neatly on the table at the end of the meal.

4. Keeping the elbows off the table.

Rules for mealtime

5. Breaking bread, rolls, muffins in small pieces before they are buttered.

6. Wiping the mouth before drinking to keep the edge of the cup or glass attractively clean.

7. Never overloading the fork.

8. Placing the fork and knife across the middle of the plate in line with the edge of the table when finished eating. The handles should be to the right, with the fork nearest the table edge, the prongs of the fork upward and the edge of the knife blade toward the edge of the table.

9. Pushing the chair back into position at the end of the meal.

Courtesy at the table

10. Asking to be excused if he must leave the table before the others leave.

11. Asking to have things passed to him instead of reaching across the table for them.

12. Never interrupting the conversation of others but waiting patiently for his turn to speak.

This brief survey of some of the important manners a child should learn before he is 10 years old is not a complete list. It is merely a guide to help parents know what they can expect of their child by the time childhood draws to a close.

"Sissy"

My 8-year-old son used to have good manners. Now he refuses to do anything polite because he claims that only "sissies" have good manners. How can I combat this point of view?

Most boys the age of your son feel as he does about good manners. They are so afraid of being labelled "sissies" by their friends that they bend over backwards to be boorish. Don't make too much of an issue of manners at this time. Insist that your son behave reasonably well at home and when there are adults present. Then let him be as boorish as his friends when he is with them. In several years, when he begins to be interested in dating girls, he will take his manners out of cold storage, polish them up, and put them to use again.

"Thank you" notes

My two children, Joan and David, aged 7 and 9 respectively, insist that they do not have to write "thank you" notes to people who give them gifts they don't like. How can I convince them they are wrong?

Tell them the notes are not so much for the gifts as for the thought behind the gift. The giver cannot be expected to know what the children will like or dislike. Therefore, it is up to the child to be gracious and polite about any gift, whether it is liked or not, because of the thought that prompted the giving of the gift. Tell your children they may receive no more gifts from anyone until they learn to accept gifts graciously. They cannot be rude to a person to suit their own whims.

Children's parties

I have always given a party for my children on their birthdays. Now that they are of school age, I find such parties increasingly burdensome because there are always some children who make a mess of the house. Yet I hate to deprive my children of the pleasure of entertaining their friends. What should I do?

If the children who have bad manners are not special friends of your children, why not omit them from your invitation list? Don't deprive your children of the fun and educationally valuable experience of entertaining just because a few of their guests are troublesome. One good way to cut down trouble is to put the troublemakers to work. When they start to get into mischief, ask them to help you pass the food, to set up equipment for games, or to prepare soft drinks. This is a good way to keep idle hands out of trouble.

Telephone manners

*What manners should I teach my children
in regard to the use of the telephone?*

Teach them how to greet people over the phone and how to end their conversations graciously. Set a time limit on the length of the call so as not to inconvenience the families on either end of the wire. Explain that it is bad manners to listen to another person's conversation over the phone or to interrupt when another person is talking over the phone except in the case of an emergency. And, finally, teach them that one should never say things over the phone that they would not be willing to say in a face-to-face conversation.

Assisting in entertaining

*When I have guests, I should like to have my
7-year-old son, Peter, help with the entertaining. How
much should a child of that age be able to do?*

You are very wise to give your son training in entertaining while he is still young and before he has become ill-at-ease and self-conscious when guests are present. At the same time, you do not want to give him this education at the expense of your guests. A boy of Peter's age should be able to be present when the guests arrive, greet them graciously, and offer to take their wraps to another room. Then let him go off to his room to read or play until time for refreshments. At that time, he can help you pass refreshments and see that every guest is taken care of. If it is then his bedtime, let him say "Good night" to the guests and go quietly to bed without disturbing you or the guests. Each year, as he grows older, he should be able to assume more responsibility when you entertain.

Nagging about manners

*My husband is constantly nagging at the children about
their table manners. This upsets the whole family
and makes meal hours a perfect nightmare. I maintain that
it is better for children to enjoy their meals than to
have good manners. Who is right?*

To a certain extent, both you and your husband are right. Children should enjoy their meals but this shouldn't mean eating like little pigs. They can enjoy a meal and eat in a mannerly way at the same time. Perhaps your husband is expecting adult table manners from your children and, when he does not get them, it annoys him to the point where he cannot restrain his reproofs.

Why not try to give your children an incentive to eat in a mannerly fashion by making a game out of good table manners? Give the whole family the "rules" at the beginning of the meal and then let every member vote, at the end of the meal, on the one whose manners were best. For the winner, there should be some reward, such as a candy bar or piece of cake. This method of getting good manners at the table will prove to be far more effective than fussing and will not take away the family's appetite as fussing is likely to do.

chapter 19

The sick child

Every child, no matter how healthy he may be, gets sick at some time or other. The sickness may be nothing but a slight cold, but precautions are still necessary to avoid further trouble. A minor illness in childhood can quickly turn into a major one if proper care is not given. When a child reaches school age, he is likely to have more illnesses than when he was at home, away from other children. Sooner or later, he will pick up germs of the typical childhood diseases, mumps, measles, and chicken pox, and he will surely get a cold when colds are spreading around the classroom.

Preparing yourself

As a parent, you should be prepared to meet any emergency. Choose a doctor whom you may call when your child is not feeling well. If the trouble is not serious, the doctor can tell you over the telephone what to do and will not suggest a home visit or an office call unless he feels it is necessary. You should also have on hand simple remedies for colds and upset stomachs. Ask your doctor to prescribe such remedies for home use.

131

Most important of all, make your own psychological preparation for your child's illness. Don't allow yourself to be upset or overanxious unless the doctor tells you the illness is serious. Children recover from illness quickly and show little if any bad aftereffect. You *cannot* tell just how sick they are from how irritable or fussy they are when ill. Usually a child is fussier when the illness is slight than when it is really serious.

Getting your-self upset won't help

And don't expect children to be able to diagnose their illness. It is impossible for them to locate pain as adults can. All they can tell you is that they are not feeling well, but they usually cannot tell you where it hurts. If *you* show concern, it is likely to exaggerate the childish fears that always accompany even the slightest physical upset.

When childhood sickness is serious

A SHORT illness is not really serious, even if it has been severe while it lasted. Prolonged illness, on the other hand, can do much physical and psychological damage to a child. It drains his strength and thus stunts his growth. Whether this stunting will be temporary or permanent will depend partly upon the length and severity of the illness and partly upon the time in the child's growth cycle when the illness strikes him. Of equal seriousness is the psychological damage caused by a lengthy illness. Many a child's personality is damaged by scars caused by unfavorable attitudes developed during the illness.

The damage of lengthy illness

For that reason, parents should watch their children's behavior closely for clues as to whether or not they are feeling up to par. See if a child seems listless, fretful, and uninterested in the things he formerly enjoyed; if he eats poorly for several meals in a row; and if he is restless during sleep. It is wise to call the doctor and report to him the symptoms you have observed. The chances of a speedy recovery are greater if the child is under a doctor's care.

Danger signals

During illness

WHILE your child is ill, you must expect him to be restless, fretful, and ill-mannered. It is wise to overlook his difficult behavior because he needs your love and attention, not discipline. Be kind and sympathetic, not scolding and fault-finding. Emotional tension always increases trouble and will keep the child from eating and sleeping well, thus prolonging his illness or making it worse. For that reason, it is important to keep him as calm as possible even though it means a temporary break in your training.

When a child begins to convalesce from an illness, he is even more troublesome than when he is really ill. He will try the patience of even the most patient parent. He will want attention constantly and complain if he does not get it; he will rebel against taking his medicine and eating the food the doctor has prescribed; he will get out of bed and play and run around; and he will complain that there is nothing to do. All of these will delay recovery, so use every possible method to avoid them.

Some things to expect

Make illness pleasant enough so that the child will not dread it—but not so pleasant that he will learn to "enjoy poor health." Of course a sick child needs more attention than a well child. But this attention should take the form of helping him to *amuse himself* rather than amusing him. Give him crayons to draw with, simple jigsaw puzzles to work, bring in a new toy or a new book, let him watch television programs he enjoys. Prepare the food he especially likes; his appetite will be poor and you will have to tease it with foods he likes best to encourage him to eat as much as he needs.

Help him help himself

Preparing the child

IF YOUR child gets an illness that will lay him up for several days, or if the hospital or an operation is necessary, *prepare him* for what is in store for him. Tell him how long the doctor says he will be sick, just what he will have to do to get well, what will happen to him in the hospital, and how long it will be before he can come home and do the things he did before he was taken sick. Even in a minor illness or injury, it is best to prepare the child for it by telling him what the treatment will be and how long it will last.

Getting cooperation

In this preparation put special emphasis on doing what the doctor or nurse says, and not making things difficult for the people who are trying to make him well. If he rebels against taking medicine or refuses to remain quietly in bed, remind him that *he* is the one who will suffer and that it may mean missing out for a long time on the good times his playmates are having. Most children will be cooperative if they are given reasons for doing what they are asked to do.

The problem of pain

Because there is always some pain connected with even a minor illness, the child should be told that his throat, his tummy, or some other part of his body will "hurt" for a time. Emphasize that doctors today know how to keep people from suffering better than they did in the past, and that if he is willing to do as the doctor says, he will not suffer long. If you are calm and matter of fact about the pain, it will go a long way toward keeping your child calm and thus preventing the increase in pain that comes with nervous tension. Ask your doctor to prescribe a sedative for times when the pain is especially severe or to enable your child to have a restful night.

Preparation for return to normal

Gradual return to normal

AFTER the child's illness has reached the turning point and he begins his period of convalescence, make his schedule as nearly normal as possible. It takes time to get back to normal psychologically just as it takes time to get back physically. That is why you must make this change-over a gradual one. Gradually limit the extra attention you gave him when he was sick, the specially prepared food and the special entertainment. Take the attitude, "Now you are better, so you can do this or that for yourself."

Most children will resist getting well, especially if life during their sickness has been especially pleasant. Don't stretch the convalescence beyond the needed time as this is likely to encourage an "invalid complex" in the child.

For a school child, convalescence should be a period of making up for lost time at school. Find out from his teacher what school work was covered during his absence and gradually help him to make up this work. Before he returns to school, all missed work should be made up so the child will return to his class without the handicap that illness so often brings.

Making up lost time

As soon as your child is well enough to play with his playmates, see to it that he learns the play skills his friends learned while he was away. If they aren't willing to take time out to teach him, or if you cannot do so, it would be a good investment to have a high school boy or girl spend some time with your child, teaching him what the other children learned during his illness. If you don't fill in the gaps, your child will find himself in the role of an outsider in play.

134

I MAGINARY illness is one of the commonest ways of escaping responsibilities and of gaining attention. The child quickly discovers that if he complains he is "not feeling well," he gains all the good features of being sick without the pain and discomfort that come with real illness. Because imaginary illness can quickly become a habit, it should be nipped in the bud as soon as there are any signs that it is beginning to be used as a means to an end. Otherwise it may grow into a deep-rooted habit and the child will actually come to believe that he is sick.

Pretending can become a habit

How can a parent tell if the child is really sick or if he is merely pretending to be? You can usually tell by his behavior. If you suspect that his illness is imaginary, suggest doing something you know your child enjoys: a movie, a trip to the zoo, or a treat of ice cream. If he suddenly gets well, you will know he is not sick. But if he says "I don't feel like it," you will know that he really is not well.

How you can find out

The reactions of older children are more guarded; you cannot always catch them unawares as you can a younger child. As a result, you cannot tell so easily if the sickness is real or pretended.

It is wise to call in a doctor or take your child to his office. He can quickly tell if there is anything the matter. This is not an unnecessary expense, as it may seem at first. One visit of this sort is usually enough to convince a child who has talked himself into believing he is sick, that there is nothing the matter with him except what he imagines there is. By doing this, you will end this form of "escape" which can and often does prove to be a handicap to a person throughout life.

If necessary, ask the doctor

Calling doctor

My husband doesn't believe in calling a doctor when a child gets sick. He claims a mother should be able to take care of a sick child. I am afraid something serious may happen some day and then he will regret his stand. How can I convince him that having a doctor during illness is a necessity, not a luxury?

E XPLAIN to your husband that you are neither a doctor nor a trained nurse and, therefore, are no more able to take care of illness than he is. Surely this will make sense to him. Read the advice given in one of the good baby books written by noted baby doctors. But if your children show any symptoms that alarm you, such as very high fever or severe pain in any part of the body, call the doctor without consulting your husband. Also, take them to the doctor at least once a year for regular physical check-ups, to be sure they have necessary vaccinations against disease, and for advice about food, vitamins, sleep, and good health care.

If you have a family doctor, he will be willing to advise you over the telephone when there is nothing seriously wrong with your children, and thus save the expense of a visit. Tell your doctor how your husband feels about medical care and he may know how to help you. But don't neglect your children's health, no matter how strongly your husband objects to medical expenses.

Home doctoring

I have had a lot of experience with sickness as I came from a large family and someone was almost always sick. I have also read many books about all phases of child care. We have a very small income and I wonder if it would be wise to try to take care of the baby I am expecting soon without the expense of a doctor.

Home doctoring can be very dangerous, and I urge you strongly not to cut down expenses this way. If every penny in your budget must count, cut down on some of your entertainments or your clothes, but *not* on medical care for your baby. Each year, as your child grows older, you will need less and less medical care for him. But to insure a good start in life, give your baby the best medical care available. This does not necessarily mean bankrupting you. All hospitals today have clinics that charge very small fees and where the best doctors of the community give their services. Don't deprive your baby of an opportunity to grow up to be a healthy adult just to save a few dollars!

Dreads shots

My 5-year-old Linda has asthma, so has had so many shots in her lifetime that she has developed a terrific fear of doctors and of having another shot. She works herself up into a panic every time she must have a shot and this makes her condition worse. How can I deal with this problem?

When your daughter is well and in a good humor, talk to her seriously about the meaning of asthma and how necessary it is at times for her to have a shot. Tell her that if she will relax and look the other way when the doctor gives her a shot it won't hurt any more than a pin prick. Looking at the needle and making the body tense with fear exaggerates what would otherwise be a very minor pain.

She is a bit young to develop a calm attitude about her illness and to be willing to try your suggestions. However, explain to the doctor how she feels about shots; he may be able to distract her attention when he gives her one. Once she sees for herself how much better it is to look the other way and relax, she may be willing to cooperate better in the future.

Keep calm yourself

Every time my baby, who is just 9 months old, gets sick,
I get so worked up that I can hardly look after him.

Yᴏᴜ must learn to control your emotions before your baby is old enough to become terrified whenever he is sick. Seeing you upset will make him think he is dangerously ill and this, in turn, will make him worse instead of helping him to get well. One very good way to keep calm is to know the different childhood illnesses: how long they usually last, the common symptoms, and the best ways to treat them. Ask your doctor to recommend a good book on baby care for you to study. Train yourself to keep calm in an emergency and treat illness in a matter-of-fact way unless your doctor tells you there is need for concern.

Neglect of family

My youngest child, who is nearly 4, is often sick. When ill Stevie
wants me to do something for him all the time, so that I
must neglect the other children. Now they have quite a hostile attitude
toward Stevie. If I don't give him the attention he wants,
he is very fretful and makes himself worse.

Yᴏᴜʀ Stevie has certainly learned to lead you by the nose. No wonder your other children resent him and feel you are playing favorites. *Now* is the time to put an end to this spoiling. When Stevie is well, see that he does not get any more than *his share* of attention. The next time he is ill, see that he is comfortable and has something to amuse himself with. But don't give him as much time as you have done in the past. He may fuss and make himself worse—but this is the penalty you must pay for pampering him in the past. It is best to take the bull by the horns now and settle the matter. If you don't, Stevie will grow up to be a spoiled brat. His brothers and sisters, and everyone he meets, will resent his bids for attention.

chapter **20**

Children
with handicaps

Parents'
attitudes—
right and wrong

F<small>OR</small> every parent whose child is handicapped in some way, the most important goal is this, I think: to recognize and accept the handicap in as calm and wise a manner as possible. Living in hopes that some miracle will overcome this handicap, even when the best medical advice is "no," is like living in a fool's paradise. With such an attitude the parents and child are doomed to bitter disappointment when the handicap persists. Even more serious, unwillingness to accept the handicap results in lack of adjustment to it, and adjustment is essential if the child is to live a happy, useful life.

Getting help

N<small>o</small> matter what the handicap, the parents' first step should always be to consult the best medical specialists about the child's condition. They can tell the parents, with reasonable certainty, what the chances are for the improvement or worsening of the condition. They can also tell what the child can and cannot do now and as he grows older, and how the parents should treat the child so as to help him to develop a healthy attitude toward his handicap.

Specialists are generally willing to adjust their fees to meet the family budget. Therefore, no family with a handicapped child should remain in the dark about the child's condition because they feel they cannot afford a specialist. If there is no one in the community with that specialty, the family doctor can recommend a specialist in the nearest community and can make all the necessary arrangements for the parents to take the child to him.

A specialist should see the child

Attitude of parents and child

THE child's attitude toward his handicap will reflect his parents' attitudes. That is why it is essential that the parents' attitudes be healthy. This means a cheerful acceptance of the child's handicap, a thankfulness that things are no worse than they are, and the belief that with strict adherence to the doctor's orders the handicap will grow no worse and may even become better. And it also means the belief that a child can live a happy, profitable, and full life, in spite of his handicap.

When parents are, on the other hand, discouraged and disheartened by the child's condition, it is impossible for them to keep their attitudes entirely to themselves. Even though they may never put their concern or their heartbreak into words, the child quickly senses how they feel and is unfavorably affected. This is just as true for brothers and sisters as it is for parents. If the handicapped child's brothers and sisters "feel sorry" for him, this will tear down all the good his parents' healthy attitude can do to build up in him an equally healthy attitude.

A child soon senses gloom

Attitude of others

CONTRARY to what people may believe, even young children are sympathetic toward a child who obviously cannot do what they do. When a child is lame, hard of hearing, suffers from a heart condition, or is rather slow in learning, children his age will not laugh at him or make jokes about his handicap. Instead, they will feel sorry for him and offer to do things when they see he cannot do them for himself. This sympathetic

139

attitude toward the handicapped becomes stronger as children grow older and have a better understanding of just what a physical or mental handicap means to a child.

Most children are considerate

Sometimes, of course, children need guidance in growing toward this understanding. Sometimes, too, one child will lead a group of others into tormenting or isolating a child who is handicapped. When this happens, it must be stopped quickly by appealing to the children within the group. Most children, fortunately, once they understand, will make a place within their activities for a handicapped child. For example, when a lame boy cannot play baseball or football, they will often make him the scorekeeper. In this way he can feel he is taking part in the game even though he cannot play.

Others will reflect a child's own attitude

Much depends, of course, on the attitude of the handicapped child himself. If he asks no special favors and is a good sport, children will accept him. If he trades on his handicaps or demands continual sympathy, children will resent this and avoid him. Eventually he will be left out of their friendship and activities. This will increase his feeling of being different and often he will blame other children and his handicap for his loneliness. Handicapped children must be guided away from falling into this trap.

Helping the handicapped child

Here are a few specific suggestions that will help the handicapped child to make good social adjustments, to be happy and useful in spite of his handicap:

1. Teach the child to *live with* his handicap. This means not only accepting his handicap but also changing his adjustment to it as the handicap itself changes.

A child can learn to live with a handicap

2. Encourage the child to learn to do what he *can* do with his handicap, even if this is not as much as others his age can do. He must realize that no one can do everything, and that what *he* can do is as great a contribution to society as what others do.

3. Help him to see he should not use his handicap as a way out of a difficult situation or to gain sympathy.

4. Teach him that getting angry with others when they offer help is unkind as it embarrasses them. Instead, he should try to accept their help graciously.

5. Help him to cultivate cheerfulness. It will not drive away pain, but it will help him to bear it.

6. Encourage him to be a good companion by being a good sport and entering into the interests of others. If he shares their interests, he will find they will try to share his interests, too.

A handicapped child can make a contribution

7. Teach him not to talk about his handicap to others unless the situation requires it. If he is asked about it, he should learn to answer in a matter-of-fact way.

8. Help him to learn not to be upset by tactless comments of others or by stares from strangers. If he can realize that most of these people are not being wilfully unkind, but only thoughtless, some of his hurt will disappear and he will be better able to cope with them.

Some things need to be overlooked

9. If he can go to a regular school, there will always be other children to help him when he needs help. If, on the other hand, his handicap makes it necessary that he go to a special school or that he have his schooling at home, he should learn to accept this as he accepts other obstacles his handicap puts in his path.

10. Avoid expecting or demanding more than his share of attention and help from his parents. He must remember that his brothers and sisters have their rights and that it is unfair for him to take over those rights. The more he can learn to do for himself, the less he will have to depend on others for help.

It's good to learn to be independent

What shall I tell?

Our only son, Johnny, is now 5. He was born crippled and has had three operations, none of which has cured him. The doctors say he always will be a cripple and can never play the games other children play. Should I tell him and, if so, when?

A 5-year-old is a trifle young to be told so grim a fact. Why not break the news to him gradually and, when he finally asks you, point-blank, "When will I be well?" tell him the truth. This is not likely to come up for several years.

In the meantime, prepare him for the bad news not only by giving him hints and suggestions that he will never be like other children but also by helping him to develop substitutes for his handicap. He may never play running games like tag, hide-and-seek, or baseball, but what about swimming? Many doctors recommend swimming for cripples. Then there are many games of intellect, such as guessing games, card games, and the so-called parlor games. Get some books describing these games and teach Johnny to play those he is able to learn. If he can play such games with other children, the chances are that he will be a part of their play group and will have as much companionship as other children.

Depressed and blue

My 10-year-old daughter had polio two years ago and is badly crippled. She used to be such an active child and loved to play out of doors. Now, whenever the weather is good, she is upset because she wants to be out doing things with the other girls. She feels so out of things and this makes her very unhappy

IT is natural that a girl who liked to play games with her friends would be blue and depressed when she knows she cannot do so any longer. But she *can* become part of the play group if you have the time to help her.

If she needs help in getting around, could you not take her to where her friends are playing? Let her sit on the side lines and watch. If they are playing some sport like tennis or basketball, she can be the scorekeeper. After the play, invite the girls to your home for a snack. In this way, your daughter will be with the girls, she can discuss their interests with them, and feel that she is again a part of the group.

Each year, as your daughter's friends grow older, they will spend less and less time on games and sports of an active type. If she can keep on being a member of the group until then, she will be less handicapped in the group activities later than she is now.

Managing alone

My son, who is just 5, was born blind. I have taken care of him day and night since his birth. At times, I feel very depressed because I wonder what will happen to him if something should happen to me. His father couldn't give up his work to care for him

EVEN though your son is blind, he must be trained to be as independent as possible. Otherwise, he would be in a bad way if something should happen to you. I suggest that you send him to a school for blind children as soon as he is ready to go away from home. Let him start as a day student at first, if there is a school for the blind near you. Otherwise, he will have to go as a boarder.

Much as you may hate to send the boy away from home, it is essential that he learn to be as independent as possible. This he will not learn so long as he remains at home and is waited on, day and night, by you. In a school specially planned for blind children, your son will be taught how to be independent. Then you will not have the worry of what will happen to him in the future as you are sure to have if he remains dependent on you.

Knowledge of seriousness

My 7-year-old daughter, Karen, was in an automobile accident. Her right arm was badly crushed and the doctors have little hope that she will ever have much use of it. They have saved her arm but it will never be normal. Should we tell her how serious it is?

A 7-year-old is a bit young to be told as grim a truth as you must tell your daughter. I suggest that you and the doctor break the news to her gradually. Start off by telling her she must learn to use her left hand as it may be a long, long time before she can use the right hand. If the doctor recommends physical therapy treatments to enable Karen to get the greatest possible use from her injured arm, see that she has these treatments at any cost and that she cooperates whole-heartedly with the therapist in the exercises. As time goes on, she will gradually sense the truth. But, by then, she will have acquired enough skill with her left hand that she will not feel the situation to be as hopeless as it seems right now.

Success despite handicap

My son is deaf, but he has learned to lipread and his teachers tell me he is very bright. He is independent and ambitious and he wants to go on to college. It would be a financial struggle, but we are willing to do without things if it would mean he could have a successful future. Is there any chance for him to succeed in business or in a career?

B Y ALL means encourage your son to get as much education as possible. At no time in our history were there as many job opportunities for the physically handicapped as there are now—but to take advantage of these opportunities, your son will need all the education and training he can get. What he will be depends on his own talents and interests, but many deaf persons are working successfully in positions where there is little need for constant communication: for example, as laboratory technicians, chemists, linotype operators, draftsmen, accountants, and in many other occupations.

Remember, too, you do not have to struggle alone. There are many organizations, private and government, that can help you with advice and training and other services. Ask your librarian for lists of these. Also ask your doctor and your son's school counselor.

chapter 21

The adopted child

IF YOU want a child and your doctor tells you that you cannot have one, why not consider seriously the possibility of adoption? If you have one child and there will never be another, why not give your child the companionship of a brother or sister by adopting a baby who has no home and who can complete the family you have always dreamed of having?

*Old notions
about adoption
have changed*

Gone are the days when people felt that a childless couple was destined to remain so because it was God's will. Gone, too, are the days when eyebrows were raised when it became known that a child was adopted and doors were literally shut in his face.

*The adopted
child's place
in the family*

Many people believe they could never feel the same toward an adopted child as they could toward one of their own flesh and blood. *But this is rarely true.* An adopted child generally receives as much love as a real child, and his position in the family is the same as that of a real child. For, in reality, he *is* his parents' child. Once they legally adopt him, they assume all the responsibilities of real parents; he has all the rights and privileges of a real child.

How to adopt a child

You cannot go out the same day you finally decide you want to adopt a baby, get one, and bring it home with you! You may have to wait for several years before you are granted the custody of a baby. And it will be one or two years more before all the legal matters are completed.

When you decide to adopt, ask your doctor to recommend an approved adoption agency. Don't try to get a baby through back-door methods and don't take a baby that someone knows about and can arrange to get for you for a sum of money. If you do, you may live to regret this haste very seriously.

A child whose adoption is arranged for by a recognized agency is thoroughly tested, physically and mentally, to make sure that he is healthy and normal. His parentage is generally known to the adoption agency, and why he is being placed for adoption. This is something you must trust the agency to investigate. You cannot expect to know the facts, because they are confidential. Furthermore, the adoption agency takes care of the legal matters connected with adoption, thus avoiding the heart-breaking experience of the baby's parents coming to claim him from his adopted parents at a later date.

Depend on an adoption agency

Period of preparation

REAL parents have nine months to prepare for the arrival of their own child. In the case of adoption, this period is generally longer. While waiting, you will be interviewed by members of the staff of the adoption agency. You will take tests to see if you are physically, financially, morally, emotionally, and intellectually equipped for parenthood. Don't be surprised if an agency worker drops in on you, unannounced, to see how you live when not expecting a visitor.

Besides preparing a room and equipment for a baby, you must prepare yourself *psychologically* for this big event. This is often more difficult than preparing for one's own baby! It means that both parents-to-be feel sure they are doing the right thing, that they will love the child as much as if he were their very own, and that they will never turn against him even if he does not come up to their dreams and hopes. To believe this, they must accept the scientifically proved fact that, if the child's physical and intellectual endowments are good, what

Heart and mind must be ready

he turns out to be is determined by his environment, especially during the early years of his life. Because they can trust a recognized adoption agency to investigate carefully the ancestry of a child, his final development therefore becomes the parents' own responsibility.

Who is the child?

$\mathbf{M}$ost foster parents would like to know who are the parents of the child they adopt. *This they should never know.* And, if the child comes from a recognized agency, they will never know, no matter how many questions they may ask. This is as it should be, and foster parents should accept this fact without reserve.

The importance of secrecy

But why, many ask, should foster parents not know who are the real parents of the child? And why shouldn't the real parents know who are the foster parents of their child? The answer is simple. So long as they do not know and have no way of finding out, any attempt to find the child and perhaps restore him to his real parents will be permanently blocked. The foster parents won't be able to blame the real parents if the child doesn't turn out as they had hoped. All the real parents will ever know is that their child is in a "good home." All the foster parents will ever know is that their child came from physically and mentally good stock.

The question of legitimacy

You will never know definitely whether the child you adopt is legitimate or not. But chances are that he is illegitimate from good parentage. That is why he is available for adoption. So, if you have strong religious or moral convictions against illegitimacy, it is better not to adopt a baby. But the circumstances of his birth have nothing to do with his potentialities. Therefore, you have no cause for concern about how he will develop, if *you* provide the child with a good environment and if *you* give him the love every child needs.

Your relatives and friends will be curious to know about the child you adopt, so you must be prepared for their searching questions. Even if you know something about his parentage, keep this a complete secret. Never tell your family or your most intimate friends. Every adoption agency advises: say you know nothing about the child's parentage. This is essential to his future happiness: you must guard the secret of his birth, if you know it, as a sacred trust.

146

THE parents of an adopted child always love the child as much as they would their very own. First, they have waited so long for a child of their own who never arrived. Then they have waited so long for a child to adopt. Their love is heightened, therefore, because the child fulfills a longed-for hope. Few adopted children ever have reason to question their *parents'* love for them.

Unfortunately, this is not always the case when there are *other* members in the family. If there are other children, born before or after the adopted child's arrival, the brother-sister rivalry and jealousy, found in almost every home, may be increased by the real child's feeling that the adopted child does not "belong" to the family. It takes tactful handling of this situation to avoid heartbreaks for the adopted child who soon feels that he is an unwanted member of the family.

Jealousy and rivalry

Members of the older generation often believe adoption is wrong because God sends children to families He believes will make good parents. Many grandmothers are prejudiced against adopted children, especially when they have real grandchildren. The adopted child is sensitive to these feelings; he feels even more unwanted and unwelcome. To avoid this unfortunate situation, parents must do all in their power to convince their elderly relatives of the joy the adopted child brings into their lives.

Prejudices of older relatives

Tell the child he was adopted

SOONER *or later every adopted child must know that he is adopted.* How he learns this, and from whom, is most important for the attitude he develops toward himself and his foster family. Learning the wrong way from the wrong source can do harm that no amount of love and care will ever undo.

There is no time like the present to inform the child of his adoption. As soon as he can understand words, he should gradually know that his parents selected him from thousands of other babies to come to live with them because they loved him and wanted him for their own. Later, as the child's ability to understand increases, the facts of adoption can be explained to him. Always, however, emphasis should be placed on the fact that his foster parents *wanted him* and that his own

What to tell the child

147

parents were unable to give him a home. By the teens, most adopted children suspect that they are illegitimate and many of them go through a period of resentment against their own parents for turning them out in the cold world instead of providing a home for them as other parents do.

Preventing heartbreaks

The adopted child must have a healthy attitude toward the whole matter of adoption, fostered by years of experience with people who love him in the home, and people in the community who accept him as they accept all other children who are not adopted. Only in this way will he escape the heartbreaks and resentments that always come to an adopted child when he realizes the full meaning of adoption. That is why it is so essential for parents of an adopted child to make sure that their child understands from them and from no one else the full meaning of adoption.

Even strangers may find out

Don't ever keep an adopted child in the dark in the hope that he will never discover he is adopted. Even when parents move far away from relatives and friends, there is always the possibility someone will learn that their child is not really their own and will tell the child. Hearing this for the first time from an outsider can be such a shock to a child that its effect may never be completely overcome—nor will the child's attitude toward his parents ever be the same again.

Children may be thoughtless

The worst possible way for a child to learn that he is adopted is from another child—yet this can happen easily. Billy may overhear his mother saying Johnny is adopted. He may not fully understand what the words mean, but this does not keep him from repeating them when he and Johnny have a quarrel. "I don't want to play with you! *You're adopted!*" he shouts. Johnny may not understand the words fully either, but still, he is hurt. Protect your adopted child by telling him yourself as only you can do to make him feel chosen and loved.

Child's parentage

Our Marie, who is 8, has known ever since she could understand, that she is an adopted child. Recently, she has been asking when she can see her real mother and father, where they live, and so on. How can I answer her questions?

Marie will make herself very unhappy if she doesn't control this curiosity about her parentage. I very much question whether you or your husband can handle the matter as well as an outsider can, because she may interpret your silence as a sign of your selfishness, or as a revengeful way of keeping her from her real parents. Why not ask your minister to talk to the child? As an outsider, he can present the facts to her in a far more impersonal way than you or your husband can.

I am sure it will be a blow to her to know that her parents voluntarily gave her up for adoption, and it may make her bitter and resentful for a time. However, you and your husband should accept this fact and do all you can to let her know how much you love her and want her. Then, in spite of all the things she may say and do to hurt you, I am confident that she will eventually get over this bitterness and show you the love and devotion of a real daughter.

Grandparents' objections

My doctor tells me I can never have children. My husband and I are very anxious to adopt a baby but my parents are very much opposed. They say they will not recognize it as their grandchild and will have nothing to do with it. Do you think they would get over their prejudice, once I had the baby?

I WOULDN'T take a chance on your parents' change of heart after you brought a baby into your home. They might soften toward the baby, while it was still tiny and cuddly, but later, when the child started to be mischievous and assertive, like other normal children, they might insist that it was the "bad blood" coming out in the child and be even more determined than they are now to refuse to have anything to do with it.

This is a case where you will have to please yourself and your husband *or* your parents. If you and he are anxious to have a child, adopt one and face the resentment of your parents. See to it that the child is with the grandparents as little as possible to avoid making the child the innocent victim of their prejudice. You might ask your minister to talk to your parents and try to make them see the matter from your angle. But don't have too much hope for success. When people grow older, it becomes harder to rid them of their prejudices.

Adopted vs. real child

We have a daughter of our own, age 6 years, and an adopted son, age 8 years. Eric feels that we prefer our daughter to him, and every time we reprove or punish him he says it's because we don't love him as much as we love Karen. How can we convince him that we do love him as much as our own child?

ARE you absolutely sure that you are as impartial toward Karen and Eric as you think you are? Because he is a boy and slightly older than Karen, he may need more discipline than she does, and you may be more severe because he is a boy and you think he can "take it" better than a girl.

Most families with a real child and an adopted child are faced by even more serious rivalry and jealousy between the children than parents find with children of their own. As a result, you must be completely impartial in your attitudes and in your discipline. You must do all in your power to let Eric know that you love him as much as Karen—but you must not overdo it or you will make Karen jealous of Eric. Nor should you pamper Eric when he needs discipline just to convince him that you love him. If you keep an absolutely impartial attitude toward the two children, Eric will eventually get over his jealousies. All children do, when they grow older and realize that their parents are not favoring any one child of the family.

Sister's child

My sister's youngest child, Nancy, has been living with us ever since she was a baby because my sister had a large family and was not well. We have no children and are devoted to Nancy. My husband is very anxious to adopt her (she is now 4 years old), but my sister refuses. What should we do?

THERE is nothing you can do but abide by your sister's decision. After all, the child is hers, and she is the only one who can grant you permission to adopt Nancy. If you insist on adopting her, you may stir up your sister to the point where she will ask to have Nancy returned to her at once. As matters now stand, chances are that she will let Nancy remain with you as long as you give her a good home and she is happy with you. You will have all the joy of parenthood, even if you have no legal claim to Nancy.

If this is not enough for you, the only thing you can do is give your sister the choice of letting you adopt Nancy or taking her back. If your sister's decision is to take her, you will have to abide by it and give up the child. Think twice before you make an issue of this matter.

chapter 22

Families are different

I KNOW three Marys whose stories can tell us a great deal about what family life means to a child. Their stories are especially interesting because the three are always together, and have a good opportunity to compare notes on family life and parental discipline and standards.

Mary Green comes from a family where both parents are young, inexperienced, and pleasure-loving. Mary's mother, having had strict upbringing, decided that *her* child would enjoy her childhood; she would be allowed to do much as she pleased. Mary's father is much too interested in his business, his golf, and his good times to bother about his child. The result? Mary is growing up like Topsy, doing just about what she pleases.

"Just do as you please"

Mary Jones is the daughter of well-to-do parents who have many outside interests and very little desire to take an active part in the child's rearing. So Mary is really being raised by a series of baby sitters of different ages, temperaments, and backgrounds. Some give her loving care and attention. Others do not.

"Mind the baby sitter"

151

Mary is getting no consistent training and has no clearly set standards of behavior to guide her.

Mary Smith, on the contrary, is brought up by her parents. They both come from strict families where the rod ruled and where children were seen but not heard. Although Mary's mother did take a course in child psychology in college, she finds it hard to give up the strict standards that were set in her own home. Besides, her husband brands more lenient methods as "new-fangled."

Family differences are important

IT ISN'T surprising that not one of the Marys is happy about her family life. And not one feels that her parents are treating her fairly! Mary Green objects to her freedom because she takes it to mean that her parents do not love her enough to do *Three families—three failures* things with or for her. . . . Mary Jones bitterly resents her parents' lack of interest and hates the parade of baby sitters who come to take care of her. . . . Mary Smith feels abused because her parents are so strict and "mean" to her.

Three unhappy Marys—and they prove the importance of family background in child-rearing methods, for how parents rear their children usually depends on how they were raised themselves. Some follow their parents' methods. Others re-act against them and do the opposite. Parents usually reflect, too, the cultural and social values they learned in childhood.

A very young child usually accepts the way he is raised without question. But when a child is old enough to play with other children, he begins to make comparisons, and then he may be actively critical of his parents and resentful. A wise parent will try to keep aware of his child's feelings and answer his criticisms.

How families differ Point out that no two families live in exactly the same way. Debby's mother works; she can't bake cookies as often as Sue's mother who stays home. Bob's father has a quick temper, but he also takes Bob fishing and to baseball games. Jill's mother rarely hugs her, but she stayed up all night to make her a costume for the play. There are five children in Don's family, so he had to help earn his new bicycle, while Mark, an only child, got his new bicycle as a birthday present.

Families differ in the way they live, in the things they expect of their children, in their forms of discipline. But this does not necessarily mean that these differences indicate they love their children more or less. A child who is loved will learn to understand this even though he may still say sometimes, "It isn't fair!" or "All the other children do it. Why can't I?"

Families differ, just as people differ, and this is one of the things that makes the world we live in interesting and exciting. But if your child seems to be always resentful and rebellious, it would be wise to examine your family through his eyes. Are you over-strict sometimes? Try to find out why he resents your actions and to help him understand the reasons for them.

Values of differences

Why families differ

FAMILIES differ from each other for many reasons, the most important of which are these:

1. *Differences in ways of showing affection for children.* Some people are more demonstrative than others by nature and by training. The quiet, reserved person is likely to give the child the impression that he or she does not love the child as much as the less reserved, more demonstrative person. Then, too, adults who have had unhappy childhood experiences or whose marriages are not happy, often make up for their own emotional defeats by lavishing affection on their children.

2. *Differences in standards for children's behavior.* What a parent expects of his child depends largely upon what was expected of *him* when *he* was a child. If, for example, the father was expected to earn money as soon as he was able to help the family finances, he in turn is likely to expect his son to do the same. The mother who, as a girl, was expected to help her mother with household duties and with the entertainment of guests will expect the same from her daughters.

From one extreme . . .

But it's a different case where parental standards were so strict that they brought about deep resentments in the child. When such a child becomes a parent, he is likely to go to the opposite extreme in the standards he sets for his children's behavior. The father who, as a child, was spanked every time he said or did anything that displeased his parents, is far more likely to be overly lenient in his discipline than is the father

. . . to the other extreme

153

whose childhood discipline was lax or *reasonably* strict.

3. *Differences in what parents expect.* What parents expect of their child depends not so much on what was expected of them when they were children as upon their own successes or failure in life. A parent who has been either a success or a failure is likely to expect more of his children than is the parent who has been merely average in whatever he undertook.

What affects parents' expectations?

The successful business man or woman, for example, or the person who has always been a good athlete, popular in social affairs, or a leader in school, college, or community affairs, will expect more from a child than he may be capable of. Similarly, the adult who has never achieved his goals but has always fallen short of what he wanted in life, is likely to set goals for his children that make up for his own lack of success—and then be disappointed when his children do not achieve these goals.

The family's rating makes a difference

4. *Differences in social and economic standing.* Families differ in amount of money, in the manner in which they live, and in their social position in the community. Material possessions and opportunities to entertain and be entertained come to mean more and more to a child each year as he becomes more intimate with people outside the home.

The child whose parents can "give him everything" proves to be a disturbing influence in a group whose parents cannot or will not give their children whatever they want. Likewise, the economic and social status of the family plays a role of great importance in determining the advantages a child may have along educational and cultural lines, and the opportunities for popularity and leadership he will have as he grows older and reaches the end of childhood.

Effect of size of family

5. *Differences in family size.* American families of today range from one child to as many as 18 or 20 children. Studies of the patterns of living and effects of family size on each individual child have shown that there is no one "ideal" size. A child from a big family has advantages and disadvantages, just as is true of the child who comes from a small family or who is the only child. However, the fact remains that the entire pattern of life in the family must change as the size of the family increases and the status of each child in the family is thus affected.

6. *Differences in family customs.* Each family has customary ways of doing things. These may range from such simple matters as ways of serving a meal to the more com-

plicated matters of celebrating holidays and observing religious beliefs. These customs, many of which are brought down from one generation to another and blended as new families are formed, determine the pattern of family life. They lend individuality to the family and add much to the feeling of belonging to that family which is so essential to a child's security.

Importance of traditions

Only when family customs differ markedly from those of his friends' families are they likely to be sources of concern, embarrassment, or even shame to the child.

Effect of differences on children

So LONG as a child is still young and his life is centered in the home, he will accept in a matter-of-fact manner the way parents do things and the way they treat him. After all, he knows nothing else. And, because his contacts with the world outside the home are limited to the few times his parents take him to other places or to see other people, he has no basis for comparison. As a result, any difference between his parents and other children's parents, or any difference between his family's pattern of living and the patterns of other families, will in no way concern him.

The world of a preschooler is his home

By the time he reaches school age and has playmates outside the home, he will begin to notice differences in the way they live and in the way their parents treat them. Soon his friends will start to talk frankly and often with exaggeration about what they are allowed to do or not do, what they have or don't have, and what they think of their parents, their parents' attitudes toward them, and the way their parents discipline them.

He begins to compare notes

To a child, being different always means being inferior. As a result of comparisons he makes with others, it is common for a child to begin to be dissatisfied with his parents, with his home life, and with his own possessions almost as soon as he starts school. This dissatisfaction gradually increases until it reaches a peak during the adolescent years.

"Why should I be different?"

As a result of this dissatisfaction, the child is unhappy and his relationship with his parents becomes increasingly worse as each month passes. He complains about everything and often convinces himself that he is unloved, unwanted, a martyr in an unhappy home. This unfortunate attitude—few children escape feeling this way at some time or other—leads to feelings of insecurity. And these, if strong and persistent, will play havoc with the child's personality and his social adjustments in the home as well as outside.

What to do about it

No FAMILY wants to lose its individuality. At the same time, no family wants its children to be unhappy because it differs in one way or another from the families of the children's friends. How can you bridge this gap between family individuality and childhood unhappiness caused by differences? I think these suggestions will help:

1. Be willing to listen to what your children have to say about their friends' families. You may get some good ideas which you can apply successfully to your own family life.

Other parents share your problems

2. Discuss with the parents of your children's friends those matters which have bothered your children. You will probably find that *they* have problems similar to yours, and that they will be only too willing to work out with you standards and rules for the children that will be similar for all.

3. Discuss problems of discipline, privileges, material possessions, and parental expectations in Parent-Teacher Association meeetings. This will give you an opportunity to hear how other parents live and how *they* treat their children. From these discussions, you may get valuable ideas on how to adjust your own pattern of family living.

Will your child be accepted?

4. Avoid trying to force your child into a social environment where children's parents are richer or more socially prominent than you. Even if you try to "live up to the Jones's," you cannot guarantee that the Jones children will accept your children on an equal footing, or that they will not make your children unhappy by flaunting their assumed superiority in your children's faces.

5. Be willing to change your points of view, your attitudes, and your pattern of life if you have reason to believe that, by doing so, you will add to your children's happiness and their feelings of pride in the family. No child can be happy in a family where he feels insecure or where he feels that his family is below the standards of the families of his friends and companions.

Family parties

*I come from a large family, always close to one another. Holidays
and most Sundays are spent with family. Now my children,
ages 6 and 8, are beginning to object to these family parties, especially
on holidays. They say none of their friends spend holidays with
"a lot of old people" and urge us to have our holidays at home alone.*

Your children don't know how fortunate they are to have relatives who are
congenial enough to have family parties. However, at their ages, doing things
like their friends and with their friends is more important than family sentiment.
You might meet them half way by allowing them to have a party in your home
for some of their friends on holiday evenings if they will go graciously to the
family celebrations. This will mean extra work for you, but you can keep the party
simple and let your children help you with the preparations.

Family meals

*I like to serve family meals in the kitchen. We eat in the dining
room only on holidays or when we have company. Recently,
Marie, who is 7 years old, has become very critical of this. My husband
is satisfied to eat in the kitchen if it makes less work for me,
and says we shouldn't let Marie dictate how we live. Do you agree?*

No, I do not agree with your husband on this point. Family living is or should
be cooperative living. This means all members of the family should make their
contributions in the form of work and suggestions. If your Marie is ashamed to
eat in the kitchen and if she would be happier to eat in the dining room as the
families of her friends do, follow her wishes if she is willing to help you with
the additional work this will mean. Let her carry the dishes to the dining room
and then back to the kitchen. Let her also help with the extra laundry this may
mean and any other additional work.

Bedtime hours

*I feel that a school child needs plenty of rest. That's why I insist that
Peter, who is just 8 years old, be in bed by 8:30 on school nights.
He says all the boys are allowed to stay up until 9 or 10 o'clock to watch
television and they think he is a "baby" because he must go to bed so early.
Am I wrong in sending him off to bed at this time?*

You are right in insisting that your son have plenty of sleep on school nights.
It is unfortunate that he has informed his playmates of the exact hour he goes to

bed. Many of them probably stay up late only occasionally but, like all children, they like to exaggerate. Why not vary your son's bed hour occasionally, especially when he has not had a too strenuous day or when there is some program on radio or television that he is anxious to hear? Then tell him to tell the boys he goes to bed at different times, sometimes early and sometimes late, depending on how he feels. This vague sort of answer will stop their labelling him "baby."

Critical attitude

> *My older son, who is 11 years old, is very critical of my husband.*
> *I admit that my husband does not take much interest in the boy and*
> *does not do things for or with him. But I cannot see why my*
> *son has taken this critical attitude toward his father.*

Y OUR son's critical attitude is a form of making up for his disappointment and feelings of neglect that arise from his father's lack of interest. He sees the other boys doing things with their fathers and he hears them talk about what their fathers do for them. Naturally your son feels somewhat like a martyr and is bitter and resentful. His criticism is an expression of this resentment. Naturally, it does not improve the relationship between father and son nor does it encourage your husband to take more interest in the boy.

Try to explain to your son that if he would stop criticizing his father and show a friendlier attitude toward him, chances are that his father would be friendlier. But try also to impress upon your husband how much he is missing by showing so little interest in his son.

Help at home

> *I believe that both boys and girls should have certain duties*
> *at home. I have given daily duties to mine.*
> *Now that they are in school, they object; they say the*
> *other boys and girls don't have to help at home. Do you think this*
> *is true or do you think they are merely trying to get out of work?*

A LL FAMILIES are different. Some require far more help from their children than others. When a family has only one child, the chances are that that child is called upon for far less help at home than is a child in a family of two, three, or more children. However, you cannot pattern your life to suit the whims of your children. If you need their help, ask for it. Furthermore, it is good training for boys and girls to learn to do household tasks. They do not have to advertise these home duties at school if their classmates think it strange that they do housework. However, I think there are few children today who do not have some home duties. If there are, it shows poor training on the part of their mothers.

chapter 23

Brothers
and sisters

ALL PARENTS want their children to get along with each other. But when there is rivalry between brothers and sisters, or friction in the form of tattling, quarreling, fighting, name-calling, or bitter jealousies—parents get upset, and family harmony is lost. How parents can prevent such unfavorable relationships between their children is a problem facing many American homes today.

Harmony—an important goal for families

Basically, the trouble between brothers and sisters can be traced to two factors: (1) parents' attitudes toward the different children in the family, and (2) parents' taking for granted that their children will be good friends and congenial playmates just because they happen to belong to the same family and live under the same roof.

Now brothers and sisters *can* be good friends. They *can* be congenial companions. But to achieve these goals, parents must use a lot of understanding, tact, and discipline. Let's look at some practical things mothers and fathers can do to develop harmony in the home and to encourage congenial relationships among brothers and sisters.

What can parents do?

Laying the foundations of harmony

THERE are five facts I think parents ought to keep in mind:

1. There will be differences in children's ages that may vary from one to ten years or more (unless the children are twins, of course). Interests, abilities, and activities in childhood depend upon the age of the particular child.

2 and 4 make trouble

Two-year-old Jane, for example, is still in the exploring stage where her main interest in all toys is examining them, pulling them to pieces, and trying without too much success to put them together again. When she tries to play with her brother, Jim, who is 4 years old, she is constantly pulling down the block houses he is building, or taking the engines off tracks just as he has his trains set up and ready to run. Is it any wonder that Jim resents being forced to play with Jane?

The gang stage

Similarly, Tommy, age 8, is just beginning to play baseball with the boys in his gang. They are a tightly knit little group and only accept outsiders when every member agrees that the new person would make a good member. Now suppose mother insists that Tommy take his little brother, Dougy, to play with the boys because she must go shopping. How will Tommy and the other boys feel?

Tommy knows the boys don't want Dougy in their game any more than he does. To them, Dougy is "just a kid" and doesn't belong. Tommy knows this, and he also knows that if he must drag Dougy along too often, he will lose status in his gang and find himself an outsider.

Children need playmates of their own age

Because children live, work, and play on different levels according to their ages, parents must recognize that each child in the family should have companionship with children of his own age from outside the home. Then when he is at home, he is likely to play and work more harmoniously with his brothers and sisters than if *all* his contacts were limited to them.

2. In any home where there are brothers and sisters, there is always more or less serious friction. This may take the form of fighting, arguing, or merely of unexpressed bitterness and opposition. Parents are not entirely responsible for this friction because every child learns, as soon as he begins to associate with people outside the home, that the role of the boy in our society is different from that of the girl. Too much home emphasis on this fact, especially when it takes the form of prohibiting girls from doing certain things because they are girls, while at the same time permitting boys to do these very

things, increases brother-sister friction. *Only when parents emphasize the fact that the role of a girl is as desirable as that of a boy, even though it is different, will brothers not try to lord it over sisters.*

3. Usually without being aware of it, *parents are prone to favor children of the opposite sex.* The mothers show partiality toward their sons, the fathers toward their daughters. This partiality leads to inconsistent discipline and granting of privileges more freely to children of the favored sex. Because the mother is with the children more than the father, there is a tendency in far too many families for girls to come out at the little end of the horn, and for the boys to feel unduly important.

Favoring the opposite sex

4. *Brothers and sisters have different abilities and different interests.* While these differences are not sharp in the preschool years, they become increasingly stronger each year thereafter as boys are fitted into the role society expects them to play and girls are molded into the feminine pattern. Only when people are old enough to have an understanding of differences in abilities and interests can one expect tolerance and understanding. This we rarely find in the attitudes of children, with the result that they take differences to mean inferiority. Thus the brother looks upon his sister as an inferior creature, while the sister regards her brother and all boys as inferior to her and her friends.

Boys vs. girls

5. *Boys have a more favorable position in our society than do girls.* Boys quickly discover this, not only at home but outside the home as well. This leads to feelings of superiority on their part and a tendency to look down their noses at all girls—and at their sisters in particular. Naturally, girls resent this attitude of masculine superiority and develop a chip on their shoulders toward all boys—and toward their brothers in particular. Much of the bickering and fighting of school age children in the home comes from a battle between the sexes where the boy has played the role of the aggressor and his sister has challenged his right to superiority.

Our society favors boys

A goal for parents

THE GOAL of every parent should not be limited to just keeping brother-sister friction down to a minimum so that there will be peace and harmony in the home. Instead, parents should emphasize the development of healthy, wholesome attitudes on the part of both boys and girls toward their own sex and toward the opposite sex. How the child gets along at home with a member of the opposite sex—whether it be a parent, a grandparent, a cousin, or another child in the family —is important. It will determine not only how well he will get along with members of the opposite sex outside the home, but also how well he can adjust to the role society will expect him to play throughout life.

Boy-and-girl attitudes begin at home

A girl who is used to being lorded over at home by her brothers will develop a chip-on-the-shoulder attitude toward all boys, and will bitterly resent the fact that she was born a girl instead of a boy. This is the type of childhood experience that gives rise to the "masculine protest" on the part of women, and which strongly works against happiness or good adjustments to marriage or any other relationship with men.

False notion of superiority is a handicap

What about the boy who has been the apple of his parent's eye because he is a boy? He is likely to develop false notions of his own superiority as well as the superiority of the male sex. This will not appreciably affect his relationship with other boys, many of whom also have these delusions of masculine superiority. But it will affect very unfavorably his relationship with members of the opposite sex—whether they be his teachers, his feminine classmates, the girls he meets in business, or the woman he courts and later marries.

Wholesome man-woman attitudes

Because healthy attitudes toward one's own sex and toward the opposite sex are so essential to good adjustments in life, parents should be constantly on guard to nip in the bud any unhealthy attitudes that may develop from their child's contacts with playmates outside the home. In the home, parents can do much to foster healthy attitudes by the way they treat their sons and daughters, and, even more important, *by their attitudes toward one another.* How can a girl or a boy who, day in and day out, throughout the childhood years, has observed the "mastery of the male sex" in every relationship between the father and mother, avoid developing an unhealthy attitude? How can a daughter think of the female sex as anything but the "weaker sex"? How can a son avoid growing up with delusions of "masculine superiority"?

Dislike for boys

My 9-year-old Sara has a strong dislike for boys and even for mature men. She has rather a cold, distant attitude toward her father whom she used to adore. I don't understand what has come over her.

Just before puberty, and your daughter is reaching that age now, most girls go through a stage of "hating boys." If brothers have teased them and acted high-handed, this dislike is generally intensified.

The less said about the matter, the better. Accept it as a part of growing up and make no issue of it, even when Sara shows a cold attitude toward her father. After she has completed her sexual maturing, I am sure you will find a marked change in her attitude toward the masculine sex. Even her brothers and father, whom she now dislikes, will seem very glamorous. Let her think what she wants about boys in general, but encourage her to keep mean and cutting remarks to herself.

Brother-sister fights

What should a mother do when her son is constantly fighting with her daughters?

A mother should punish her son for fighting with her daughters, if the son has started the fights. If, on the other hand, the daughters have started the fights, *they* are the ones who should be punished. This punishment can take the form of sending them off to their own rooms and not allowing them to play with any-one, in the home or outside, until they promise not to fight again. If they break that promise, off they should go to their rooms again, but for a longer time. This will eventually convince them that fighting is to their disadvantage and they will stop it. You cannot hope to have your son play with your daughters because boys rarely play well with girls after they pass the kindergarten age. Still, they must learn to live and let live and not constantly tread on each other's toes.

Play with girls

Johnny, who is 5, plays so well with his two older sisters that he never wants to play with the boys. I am glad, because the boys in our neighborhood seem so rough and boisterous that I do not want Johnny to be like them.

You are making a great mistake by encouraging Johnny to play so much with his sisters and by discouraging his following the pattern of other boys. If you don't encourage him to start at once to play with the other boys and to do what they do, the boys at school may label him a "sissy" and won't have anything to do with him. In a year or two from now, the girls won't want to play with him either. Then where will poor Johnny be? He will be a very lonely little boy and will develop feelings of inferiority because of his reputation of being a "sissy." It is fine that he gets along well with his sisters, and this makes life easier for you—but too much of this is a bad sign. It would be far better for Johnny to begin to follow the pattern of the average boy, even if it means a certain amount of friction with his sisters.

Baby brother

We have four daughters and had always hoped for a son. Last year, our hopes were fulfilled with the birth of David. Our daughters adore him and treat him as if he were a doll. I am so happy, as I was afraid they would be jealous of him.

You may be living in a fool's paradise. Don't conclude that all is well between your daughters and David just because he is like a doll to the girls, now. Several years from now, when he is no longer a cuddly baby, but a demanding, mischievous boy, you may find a marked change in your daughters' attitudes toward him. Furthermore, it will not help the situation to have David the apple of your eye. No matter how much you may have longed for a son, try to keep that longing to yourself. It certainly won't help the boy to know that he is your favorite, and it won't help the girls if they feel that they do not mean as much to you as David does.

A baby brother can be a real troublemaker in the home. This you may never appreciate fully until your girls are old enough to have dates. You can avoid future storms between them and David if you begin treating him as though he were the *fifth* son, not the only son.

Boy's scoffing

My son, who started school this fall, used to play very nicely with his sister who is just 18 months younger. Now he refuses to play with her and scoffs at everything she does. There are no boys in our neighborhood his age so he has no playmates. How can I get the two to play together as they used to?

Now that your son is in school, he has developed the attitude held by the other boys that boys should not play with girls. I doubt whether you can convince him that he would have fun if he would play with his sister as he used to, and I very much question whether it would be wise to try. As a school boy, he should be playing with other boys and learning to do what they do instead of playing with girls. Could you not arrange to invite some of his classmates to your home to play with him, and arrange to take him to the other boys' homes?

As for the scoffing, you should put an end to it. Tell your son he does not have to play with his sister, but that he may not scoff at her. After all, she has just as much right to play as he does. Just because girls play differently than boys does not mean that boys should make fun of them.

Complaints about being a girl

Doris, who is our only child, is constantly saying she wishes she were a boy and that she had a brother. Would it be wise to adopt a boy?

ANY child you would adopt would be so young that he would be no real companion for Doris. Are you sure that you have not nourished her desire to be a boy by saying that you would like to have a son? She may readily take this to mean that you are dissatisfied with her sex.

It is too bad for a girl to go on being sorry for herself just because she is a girl. This makes her unhappy, but, even more seriously, it interferes with good adjustments to her own sex. If she continues to complain about being a girl, the next step will be to look down her nose at everything the other girls do, and this certainly will not make her popular. Try to convince her that there is nothing wrong in being a girl—in fact, it is a very desirable thing. Let her see what role women play and how much better off women of today are than when her grandmother was a girl.

chapter **24**

Every child needs love

PARENTS used to be told, "Don't show your love for your children—it will spoil them. They will never let go of your apron strings."

Those days are over. Now we recognize that all children, no matter what their age, need love. They need love, not just once in a while, but constantly and consistently. This doesn't mean that children should be fondled and kissed all the time, of course. *It means that a child should never have any doubts about the fact that he is loved and wanted, no matter what he says or does.*

The love a child needs

Love gives a child the feeling of belonging and of security so essential to his happiness and to good adjustment to people both in and outside the home. When a child feels, for one reason or another, that he is not loved and not wanted by his parents or by his brothers and sisters, he is an unhappy child. He develops a chip-on-the-shoulder attitude which affects his behavior in the home as well as outside. And he carries over his resentments at not being loved by his family to outsiders who are in no way responsible for his feelings.

The child who feels unwanted

166

Have you noticed what happens to children who are brought up with cold, unresponsive parents? These children find it hard to respond to others. They haven't lived in a home atmosphere that encourages them to love others. The result is that people respond to them in the same cool, aloof manner as the children have been accustomed to respond to their parents. This pattern, once it is set, works against strong and lasting friendships and interferes with happiness in marriage during adult years.

Coldness can't bring happiness

Love has many forms

Love changes form as the child grows older. If it didn't change, it would likely bring irritation and embarrassment to the child. Let's look at these changes and see why this is so.

Baby wants to be held, fondled, hugged, and kissed. The warmth of contacts with others gives him the feeling of security which is essential to happiness during the first two or even three years of life. But as a toddler, he will show less interest in these demonstrations of affection and will often try to escape from your embrace or turn his head when you want to kiss him.

The change from baby to toddler

By the time he is of school age, any show of affection of the sort he formerly liked is rebuffed. It angers and embarrasses him to be kissed by anyone, even in the privacy of his own room, and he likes to show his open contempt of all outward expressions of love. When, for example, he sees a love scene at the movies, he will mock the players and openly show scorn for such "silliness." Any name of endearment—"lamb," "sweetie," and so on—which he formerly accepted in a matter-of-fact manner he now detests and does not hesitate to let his family know he is "too old" for such a name.

A school child rejects outward display of love

This, of course, does not mean that you should stop loving your child just because he is embarrassed and irritated by your expressions of affection. On the contrary, your love is as important to him when he is a school child as it was when he was a helpless baby. But *the form of expression your love takes must change to meet the more mature needs of a growing child.*

How, you ask, can a parent know when to change the *form* of his love for the child? The answer is that you must take your clues from your child's behavior. No two children are alike in this respect, any more than they are alike in other

167

respects. Therefore, you cannot set definite ages at which you should change the way in which you show your love for your child. His reactions to your expressions of love will tell you if these expressions are meeting his needs or if he has outgrown them and is now ready for more mature display of love.

*How to show
your love
is the problem*

If you don't take the clue to modify your behavior, you are likely to cause such resentments in your child that the pleasant relationship that formerly existed between you and your child will weaken and a serious gap between you and him will form. Just at the time when he needs your help and confidence the most, he is likely to feel the furthest away from you. Because it is hard for a parent to continue to love a child who shows repeatedly that he does not want the parent's love —at least not in the form it is being expressed—the parent is likely to make the mistake of feeling that the child is no longer in need of love and hence does not show him love as he formerly did.

How do you show your love?

How can a parent show his love for his child except by the usually accepted forms of fondling and kissing? Is there any other way to show real and sincere love except by close bodily contact with the loved one? Yes, there *are* other expressions of love—ones which meet the needs of an individual at certain stages of his life even better than the usual ways. Here are a few of the many ways a parent can let his child know that he loves him without kissing, hugging, and fondling him at an age when such demonstrations bring embarrassment and irritation to a child:

*Parents can
show their love
in many ways*

1. *Showing an Interest in His Affairs.* To a child, a sincere interest in his affairs, especially when it has none of the signs of "prying," is a far more effective way of showing love than any other single way. The parent who is interested enough in his child to listen to his tales of woe with the same sympathetic concentration as to his tales of triumph, shows the child that he means a great deal to his parent and that his joys and sorrows are shared by his parent.

*Interest—but
not prying*

2. *Willingness to Listen to His Problems When He Wants to Discuss Them.* The parent who is so busy with his own affairs that he never seems to be available when the child needs

the parent most, creates the impression in the child's mind that his love is very shallow. By contrast, take the parent who is ready to drop what he is doing and give his undivided attention to the child when it is apparent that the child has something which is important to him that he wants to discuss with his parent. Such a parent makes the child feel that he is truly loved and secure in his parent's affections for him.

Taking time to listen

3. *Attempts to Make the Child Happy.* A parent can plan things to give his child happiness and be willing to sacrifice his own interests to enable his child to have pleasant experiences. In this way he shows a love for the child that means more in the long run to both parent and child than demonstrations of affection which the child rejects as "babyish."

4. *Willingness to Give the Child Advantages.* Giving a child educational, social, and cultural advantages which will help him to get along successfully in life, is one of the most sincere forms of love a parent can give his child. Few parents can give their child such advantages without personal sacrifices in the form of time, energy, or money. When the parent is willing to make such sacrifices, the child quickly discovers how much his parent loves him.

Sacrifices are not wasted

Love must be continuous and consistent

Love that will mean what it should to a child must never be a hit-or-miss affair. Nor should it be given to the child at the whim of the parent and dependent upon the parent's feelings at the moment. To be a source of security and happiness to a child, *love from his parents must be consistent and continuous.* No child will believe that his parents really love him if they tell him, in a fit of temper when they are angry, that they don't love "naughty boys." Likewise, a kiss or hug, followed several minutes later by a slap or a spanking will not convince a child that his parent loves him. He must see evidence of his love for him, *even when he is naughty and troublesome.*

Rain or shine, love must go on

To convince the child of the parents' love for him, parents must plan their discipline in such a way that the child will learn to behave properly while, at the same time, avoid developing a feeling that his parents are no longer interested in him or don't love him as they did when he was younger. This can be done by putting emphasis on the *act* rather than the child. This means, don't tell your child that *he* was naughty

169

or that you are disappointed in *him*. Rather, emphasize the fact that he did a naughty thing and you hope this will never happen again because it will mean that you will have to give him the punishment that goes with that form of naughtiness.

Don't let your moods interfere

Be ready and willing to listen to what your child wants to ask you or tell you at the time it is uppermost in his mind. This will help to make him feel that he is important to you at all times, not just when you are in the right mood. When a parent loves a child, he will never be so busy with his own interests and affairs that he will not be able to give his attention to the child when the child needs and wants his attention. Can you blame a child for wondering if his parents love him when they put their own interest and activities ahead of him time after time?

Another way in which parents can show a continuous, consistent love for their child is to show appreciation for his efforts at all times, even when his achievements may be disappointing. An over-critical attitude, or fault-finding when the child's work in school or on the athletic field does not come up to parental expectations will raise the question in any child's mind of how much his parents really love him.

Children need understanding

And, finally, understanding and sympathy must be ever-present in the parent-child relationship if the child is to be convinced of his parents' love for him. This means, never ridicule his fears, never pass over his problems as trivial when you see they are important to him, and never debunk his joys or sorrows as exaggerated and not worth all the excitement they are causing him.

What about love from others?

K NOWING that he is loved by his parents is not enough for any child. When there are brothers and sisters in the home, he must feel that *they* love and understand him, too, if his position in the home is to be a secure one. Far too often, rivalry and jealousy between brothers and sisters break down the feelings of security established by parental love. This is something we parents sometimes overlook, especially when we feel sure our own relationship with the children is a sound one.

Obstacles to security

No child can feel that his position in the family is secure nor can family life be happy for him if he is constantly facing the taunts and bodily attacks of a jealous brother or sister.

170

Likewise, he will not find happiness and contentment in a home where his play is constantly interrupted by a brother or sister who takes his toys or who breaks what he has struggled so hard to build up. As he grows older, if name-calling and teasing are the common experiences when he is with a brother or sister, how can he feel happy and secure in his home? Or, if a brother or sister tattles on him and he has reason to believe that a parent heeds the tattling, will this not undermine his secure position in the family?

A job for parents

While it is hard to prevent some of the rivalries and jealousies that are inevitable in every home where there are several children, parents will do well to bend over backwards to prevent as many of these experiences as possible. A friendly, cooperative spirit can prevail in the home if parents show no favoritism or partiality toward any child, and if they do not permit rivalries to exist. Family harmony is the only way in which every child in the family can feel that he is loved and that his position in the family is a secure one.

Grandparents may be problems

Grandparents and other relatives are also important factors in promoting happiness and security for a child. They play especially important roles in a child's life if they live in a child's home or if they come in constant contact with him at family gatherings or in visits to the homes of relatives. Grandparents frequently are highly critical of young children and do not hesitate to voice their disapproval of the child's behavior. This disapproval is taken by the child to mean that his grandparents do not love him, and thus it is not surprising that he feels ill-at-ease when he is with them.

Acceptance by other children means a lot

When a child is old enough to play with children outside the home and later to attend school, being accepted by them is his sign that they like him. While children rarely show any demonstrations of affection for one another after they are 3 or 4 years of age, just being accepted by another child and being wanted in the play group is enough to convince him that the other children like him.

The child who, for one reason or another, is unpopular with other children and who discovers that they do not want to play with him, is not only an unhappy child, but also an insecure one. He may try to make up for lack of love from his playmates by clinging to a parent who loves him or he may withdraw from all human contact as much as possible and live in a daydream world where "everyone" loves him and wants him. Or he may show affection for some pet animal and derive enough satisfaction from the pet's devotion to him to make up for lack of affection from humans.

When a child feels that his parents, brothers, sisters, relatives, and children of his age dislike him, he is a bitterly unhappy child. To compensate for his unhappiness and to show others that he does not care how they feel about him, he often turns to mischievous behavior. By annoying others through his naughtiness, he has some satisfaction for lack of their love. Most adults do not understand what is back of childish mischievousness and naughtiness, and they become angry and punish the child. This merely intensifies the child's belief that he is unloved and, as time goes on, paves the way for juvenile delinquency.

Unhappiness often leads to trouble

A child's expressions of love

WHILE a child wants to be loved by others, he rarely demonstrates his love for them in a manner that they interpret as love. He may, when he is young, kiss and hug the people he loves willingly and without embarrassment, and he will usually do so when asked. Nevertheless, his demonstrations of affection are occasional and not at all consistent. By the time he is old enough to go to school, he regards such demonstrations as "sissy stuff" and refuses to kiss even his parents when anyone is around who might tease him, or when he feels that such behavior is beneath his dignity.

Children don't always show their love

Just because a child does not express his love for others in the usual adult manner does not mean that he lacks affection for them. On the contrary, he has his own ways of showing his affection, and these methods are as meaningful to *him* as the accepted adult methods are to *them*.

A child's way of loving

He wants to be with people he likes, whether they be parents, grandparents, brothers and sisters, playmates, or a pet animal. He feels secure and happy in their companionship and he likes to talk to them and do things with them. The people he loves he goes to with his troubles and with his joys. He feels secure in their sympathetic understanding and help. And he enjoys sharing with them the things that make them happy. These are a child's ways of showing he loves a person, and these ways are as meaningful to *him* as parents' ways are to *them*.

Spoiling child

I have always felt that too much love spoiled children and,
as a result, I have always tried to be impersonal in
my contacts with my children. Have I made a mistake?

Too much love, if it is of the right kind, never spoiled anyone. Selfish love or love that is inconsistent and shown only at the whim of a parent, will, on the other hand, spoil any child. By being aloof with your children, you are creating in their minds the impression that you are not interested in them. This, in turn, takes away the feelings of security that the emotional warmth of love should give.

Begin now to let your children know how much you love them. How you will show this love will depend upon their ages. You can quickly tell, from the way they react to your expressions of love, whether they are too old for such expressions. If so, modify your behavior accordingly. The important thing is to make sure that they *know* you love them.

Jealousy of baby

We have an adorable 3-month-old baby. Our first child is getting
very jealous of the baby. She says I love him more than I do her. I admit
I kiss and fondle the baby more than I do Mary but I tell
her she is a big girl now and doesn't need kisses as babies do.

You are wrong: "big girls" need kisses and other demonstrations of love as long as they want them. Your Mary is not too big to be shown how much you love her so long as she resents your demonstrations of love for the baby. You will do well to give Mary her full share of kissing and other expressions of your love. Don't reserve them all for the baby unless you want to have a bad situation on your hands. Mary will develop a deep resentment against the baby and against you, if you follow your present tactics, and this will make her into a bad little girl who will be hard to love.

Love for pet

Our son, Timothy, is 8 years old. He hasn't shown us any
love since he started to go to school but he is constantly hugging
and kissing his pet dog. This, I am afraid, makes me a little
bit jealous as I love Timothy dearly and rather resent his love for his dog.

You needn't resent Timothy's love for his pet dog if your only reason for believing that he no longer loves you is that he doesn't kiss and hug you as he did when he was a little boy. Timothy is too big a boy now to want to kiss his parents. It would be considered "unmanly" by other boys and Timothy is well aware of how they would feel. Accept this change in him as part of growing up. So long as he is friendly and happy at home, comes to you with his problems, and is willing to follow your advice, you know he loves you. Let him kiss his dog as much as he likes. It is a substitute for the love he would like to show you and his father if he did not think he was "too old" for it.

Criticism and love

My children always say I don't love them any more when I criticize or reprove them for something naughty they have done. Can't a parent discipline a child without being accused of not loving the child?

O F course a parent can discipline a child without making the child feel that the parent no longer loves him. It is the *way* the discipline is handled that creates the impression that the parent no longer loves the child. When you criticize or punish, do you become cross, fault-finding, and disagreeable about the matter? Do you allow your emotions to govern what you say or do, or do you remain calm and impersonal? Do you accuse the *child* of being "naughty" or "bad," or do you refer to *what he does* as "bad"? This difference may, on the surface, seem trivial, but I can assure you that it is not trivial. It makes all the difference in the world to a child to know that his parents love him even when he does something that must be criticized and punished.

Importance of love

Why is it so important to a child to know he is loved? There seems to be so much stress on this point nowadays. Surely a child must know that his parents love him.

Y ou cannot take for granted that a child will know that his parents love him. As a matter of fact, some parents do not love their children. A child can know that his parents love him only if they *tell* him so repeatedly and if they *show* their love repeatedly through their actions.

As for the present-day emphasis on a child's knowing that he is loved: this has come from studies that reveal how damaging lack of love or the wrong type of love is to a child's personality and to his adjustments to people. When a child finds that he is not loved, or when he is in doubt about the matter, he may do one of two things: (1) he will withdraw into his shell and live in his own day-dream world where he will get the love he feels has been denied him in real life. Or (2) he will become an aggressive, demanding, resentful person who will make people dislike him because of his unpleasant behavior. As time goes on and the child is more and more certain that he is unloved, he will have such an unattractive personality that no one will want to have anything to do with him.

Love and overprotection

I have only one child, a son. I love him so dearly that I sometimes wonder what would happen to me if anything happened to my boy. Is this bad for him?

Too much love, of the type you have for your son, is a selfish love. You are so anxious to keep something from happening to him that you are overprotecting him and this, in turn, will make him overly dependent on you. As he grows older, he will literally be afraid of his shadow and will depend so much on you or some other adult that he will be unable to stand on his own feet and take his place in the world.

Try to convince yourself that there is no more likelihood of anything happening to your son than to any other child. So long as you are reasonably careful of him, and so long as you train him to take reasonable precautions in life, his chances of living to a ripe old age are as great as those of the next child.

"No one loves me"

My 9-year-old son is constantly saying, "No one loves me." His father says Bobby is just bidding for attention, but I think the child really means what he says. Should I take him seriously or ignore it as his father believes I should?

When a child is constantly saying that no one loves him, he has a deep-rooted belief that he is unloved. It is not wise to ignore this or to assume that it is a bid for attention, as it may actually be. Instead, try to find out from the boy *why* he thinks no one loves him. Ask him if he does not know that you and his father love him, and whether he hasn't good friends among his classmates at school. You can tell, from the way he talks about this matter, where the belief has come from and whether it is sincere or merely a bid for attention.

If it is sincere, it is most important for you to get at the root of the trouble and try to find out why the child feels as he does, whether his feeling is justified or not, and then try to convince him that people do not dislike him as he believes. It is very bad for a child's personality development to believe that he is unloved. It develops in him an undesirable attitude toward himself and toward other people. This, in time, will color his behavior to the point where people will not like him.

Nickname

We have called our only child "Dolly" ever since she was a baby. Now she is 10 years old and says it embarrasses her to have us call her "Dolly", especially in front of her friends. She wants us to call her by her real name, Cynthia. Should we change?

WHEN a child is embarrassed by a nickname, parents should comply with the child's request and call her by her real name. Your Cynthia probably does not resemble a doll in any way if she has now reached the chubby stage that normally comes before puberty. As a result, she has doubtless had a lot of teasing by her classmates. Why not ask everyone you know to call her "Cynthia" and also speak to her teacher about the matter? It may take some time for you and everyone who has known her as "Dolly" to break the habit and call her by her real name, but make the effort for your daughter's sake.

This experience should be a warning to other parents who have given their children nicknames of endearment to stop using these names when the child is old enough to go to school. Such a name may seem all right to parents, but you can be sure it will serve as a good way for other children to rib a child who bears such a name.

Love as compensation

I was a successful business woman when I married. I had not planned to have children, but one arrived. At first, I was very upset as I knew it would end my career. Now I am devoted to our little daughter but I get very annoyed at her. Does this mean that I really don't love her?

BEING annoyed at a child when she is naughty or troublesome is a perfectly natural reaction on the part of any parent. However, in your case, are you sure that back of your annoyance is not some trace of the resentment you had when you knew you were having a child? And are you sure that your devotion to the child now is not more a feeling of duty and cloak for guilt because of your early resentment than a true love for the child?

Many women who do not want to have a child become "devoted" mothers, not because of a real love but to compensate for a feeling of guilt at their earlier reactions toward their children. This "compensatory love," as it is called, is an unsteady, unreasonable, and often too intense type which does a child more harm than good. You will do well to analyze your feelings for your daughter in an unbiased way, and try to discover what they *really* are.

Father's indifference

My husband is very indifferent to our daughter. Linda is 6 years old and is beginning to resent this, especially as she compares herself with her brothers, whom my husband adores. I try to make up for my husband's indifference by doing all I can to make Linda feel loved at home. Is this enough?

It is never enough for a child to be pushed aside by one parent and then have the other parent lavish affection on her as a compensation. By his indifference, your husband will destroy all the good you do. Furthermore, too much love, and that is what you are giving Linda, is not good for any child. Another side of the picture is that Linda's brothers will likely be indifferent to her, in imitation of their father. As a result, Linda will have love only from one member of her family, you. Can you not show your husband how unfair he is to Linda and what a bad example he is setting the boys?

Resentment of kissing

I have long since learned that when a child has reached the school age, kissing embarrasses him. But my mother insists upon kissing my two children, 7 and 9 years of age, even in front of their playmates. As a result, they have developed a strong dislike for her and don't want to be around when she comes to our home.

You can hardly blame your children for feeling as they do about their grandmother or resenting her demonstrations of affection in the presence of their friends. They have doubtless had to stand a lot of teasing from their friends and they want to avoid this in the future, if possible.

Try to work on your mother: convince her that children resent being kissed in public and that they become so embarrassed that it makes them want to run away and hide. Surely your mother is not so old that she cannot remember how she felt when she was their ages. If she refuses to follow your suggestions, then try to control the situation so that she will have no opportunity to greet them with a kiss when their friends are present.

Every child
needs security

YOUR child's security means more than three good meals a
day and a roof over his head. True, those are important to a
child—but he needs *emotional security* as well as security in
material things. This emotional security can come only when
he has favorable relationships with the people of his narrow
world. And he must be able to feel that he not only is an accepted member of the different groups of people with whom
he comes in contact, but also that they love and respect him
as an individual.

Too much security can be just as bad for a child as *too*
little. First, let's look at *too much* security. When his pattern of
living is so fixed that variations rarely occur, or when his rela-

Dangers of too
much security

tionships are with few people who are close to him in blood
ties so that he is sure of reasonable acceptance by them, he is
likely to be upset when any change does occur in this well-
patterned life. Never having learned to adjust to changes, he
now finds the props knocked out from under his secure little
world. He is left in a state of emotional turmoil.

The child whose life offers *too little* security, on the other hand, usually becomes a timid, scared, insecure individual who clings to anyone or anything that offers him the security his own life lacks. Sometimes he becomes aggressive and demanding, in the hope of thus gaining the security he needs to make him happy. No matter what form his insecurity takes, it leaves a mark on his personality that will cling to him throughout life in one form or another, and that will lead to poorer social adjustments than he would have made if his childhood days had offered him more security.

*Danger of too
little security*

The right amount of security

Cᴀɴ parents tell if they are giving their children the right amount of security, or too much, or even too little? No formula will fit all children because children are different in their security needs, just as they differ in all other needs. You can tell, however, by the child's behavior if he has enough security *for him.*

A child who is not getting enough security to meet *his* needs is shy, demanding, a clinging vine. He needs constant attention to keep up his morale, and he is afraid to stand on his own two feet without help from someone else. Obviously, such a child feels insecure and needs more security than he has been receiving. When there is *too much* security for the child's own good, he will show it by a poised, happy outlook on life which will crumble when anything new, different, or strange is introduced into his life. Neither type of child, therefore, has the right amount of security for his needs.

*When there is
too much or
too little*

The child who has *adequate* security, by contrast, is happy and is well adjusted to all types of people and situations. He remains unruffled in emergencies, and accepts the good with the bad with equal poise. He may, of course, be upset occasionally when the props are knocked out from under him and he finds himself falling flat on his face. But he quickly picks himself up, brushes off the dust, and is ready to tackle the next obstacle with a happy smile and the confident attitude of "I will win this time."

*When there is
enough*

The kinds of security children need

Tᴏ ᴀᴄʜɪᴇᴠᴇ the goal of a happy, well-adjusted personality, the child needs security not only in material things but in many other areas of his life. If you put too much emphasis on one type of security and too little on others, you undo all the good that comes from security. Of what value is it to a child, for example, if his parents give him a luxurious home in which to live, servants to wait on him hand and foot, and any material possession he may wish for—if they pay little attention to him and deprive him of what he wants and needs most: their love, their interest in his affairs, and their companionship?

Luxury is not security

No, the "poor little rich boy" is not to be envied, even though the things he owns may make him the envy of the children with whom he is permitted to come in contact.

To develop a child's well-rounded personality and to give him a happy childhood, parents must provide the following types of security:

1. *Material Security.* It is not necessary for a child to come from a wealthy family, or to have everything his heart desires, to feel happy and secure. What he has, however, should be *his*, not something shared with other members of the family to the point where he feels he has no real claim on it. It is important, also, that the family be in a rather secure financial position. If financial setbacks occur, it may be best not to tell a child: He may be still too young to understand that, so long as his father is in good health, there is every chance that the tide will turn sooner or later.

A feeling of ownership

If the breadwinner dies, the remaining parent should make every possible effort to give the children material security, even if it means living in smaller quarters and making other sacrifices.

2. *Environmental Security.* Whenever possible, a child should grow up in the same home with the same room, the same neighborhood, and the same school. Moving from place to place, breaking old ties and forming new ones only to break them again just as they are becoming firmly established, gives any child a feeling of not belonging anywhere.

Roots bring security

If, for business, health, or other reasons, the family must pull up stakes and move to another community or another neighborhood, all possible efforts should be made by the parents to help the children get their roots into the new environment as swiftly as possible. This can best be done by taking the old, familiar furnishings and pictures to the new home, by making the child's room look as much like his old room as possible, and by helping him to become acquainted with the new people in the neighborhood and school.

3. *Security of Child's Status in the Family.* A child must know where he stands in the family group and be sure of his position, with all the rights, privileges, and responsibilities that go with that position. Whether he is the oldes⁺, the youngest, or one of the middle children of the family makes little difference. The important thing is that he know what his position is and that the other members of the family recognize, respect, and treat him according to his position within the family group.

4. *Security of Status in the Community.* Just as is true of status in the family, the child must be secure in his position in the community if he is to be happy. He must feel that other children, teachers, and neighbors like him and accept him as one of their group. Not being accepted by the children, or feeling that he does not belong to a neighborhood group, makes a child want to withdraw from these groups because he feels the members are hostile to him. Even when his position in the family is clear and secure, it is not enough to make up for an insecure position outside the home.

5. *Moral Security.* Well-defined and consistent discipline, with clear-cut rules and regulations to guide his behavior, are essential to a feeling of security in the way a child behaves. If things that were right yesterday are condemned as wrong today, how can a child know what to do? How can he feel secure about his behavior?

When feelings of insecurity develop in a child, due to ignorance of what is right, or to faulty discipline in the home and school, the child feels so uncertain of himself and of his status within the group that he often does things to attract attention to himself and to win the favor of others who can give him the feeling of security he now lacks. The result is a troublesome, mischievous child who, as time goes on, may develop into a "problem child" or, later, even into a juvenile delinquent. By contrast, the secure child is rarely troublesome and rarely presents serious problems for his parents or teachers.

6. *Religious Security.* Unfortunately, too many children today are given religious instruction of a piecemeal sort. They pick up fragments of information at home, at Sunday school, from their friends, from their reading, or from adult conversations. Is it any wonder, under such conditions, that they lack religious security? To complicate matters further for them, they hear their friends say that they believe this or that, and that their church allows this or that, which may directly contradict what the child himself has learned. Later, as he begins

school, he is very likely to discover that some of his studies contradict what he learned in Sunday School or at home.

Religious support

How in the face of such inconsistencies and uncertainties about what is right or wrong, true or untrue, can a child have security in the area of his life where security should be the utmost importance to him? Even when he turns to prayer in the hope of meeting some of his problems, he often finds his prayers do not bring the solution he seeks. As a result, one of the props on which he was told to rely is now knocked from under him.

How can we build security?

Because security in all areas of a child's life is essential to the development of a child's personality, his adjustments to people, his work and his play, and his happiness in life what can a parent do to help his child acquire this security? Is it something a parent can do for a child or must the child get his own security? Can security acquired with the help and guidance of others be *real* security or will it vanish into thin air when the child is later forced to stand on his own two feet, without the guidance and help he has been accustomed to receive from others?

Help the child to learn to feel secure

The answers to these questions can be summed up, I believe, with this simple statement: *a child must learn to be secure, and this learning, like all other learning, will come best when the child is guided and helped by those more experienced than he.* As he gradually learns to meet his problems and to feel confident in his ability to meet new problems as they arise, he will need less and less help from others.

But until he gets enough experience of his own to be self-reliant, let's not expect him to meet problems without help. Expecting him to do so is one of the surest ways to undermine any self-confidence the child might have. And, when self-confidence is lost, the child's feeling of security vanishes.

How parents can help

Here are some of the ways parents can help their children to build up feelings of security:

1. *Make sure that your child knows you love and respect him as an individual.* Show a genuine interest in him, his interests, and his activities. Be willing to help with his problems; share his joys and sorrows with him. Even when he is troublesome and naughty, don't even hint that you do not love him.

He will be far less troublesome if he feels secure in your love than if he has any reason to doubt that you love him.

2. *Provide security in your child's life.* Unless marriage becomes unbearable, do not think of separation and never talk about it in front of the child. Let him know that he will have a home and two parents who love him and want to be with him. Only when conditions demand it should you move from place to place during the child's growing years. Let him get his roots into the ground and keep them there until they are well established.

3. *Try to provide financial security for your child.* This does not mean a large income or luxurious living. Even if it means hard work for the parents and pinching and scraping, it is best for a child to know that he will always have a roof over his head, three meals a day, and some of the things his friends have.

Freedom from want

4. *Provide security in his home relationships.* If conditions make it essential that you turn over your child's care to another person, be sure that you choose a person who will make a satisfactory substitute for you. When you employ baby sitters to stay with him, get a person you can rely upon, one who will make him happy and secure in your absence, and one who will be willing to come to you time after time, should you need her help. A child who is brought up by a succession of different people very often develops a feeling of insecurity because different people expect different things from him.

5. *Have a happy family life and happy relationships with everyone in the family.* There will be times, in every family, when members disagree and are angry with one another. These, however, should be kept to a minimum and happy relationships restored as soon as possible. A child who grows up in a happy home environment can weather many of the storms outside the walls of the home because he knows he can return to the warmth and security of the home when life outside becomes too difficult for him to cope with successfully.

Home should be a haven

6. *Provide a place in his community for him.* If your child feels insecure in school, try to find out why from his teachers, then help him to overcome this feeling. Likewise, when he is old enough to play with other children outside the home, keep a watchful eye on his play and help him to learn to play with other children in such a way that they will want to play with him. You can do a lot to help him establish himself in the play group of the neighborhood by planning pleasant play experi-

Help him find a secure place

ences for the neighborhood children in your home or back yard, and by seeing to it that everyone has a good time when they are with your child.

7. *Plan a program of discipline that will enable your child to know what he may and may not do—and be sure that every member of the family, including the child himself, understands these rules.* One lenient parent can do more harm than the good that comes from the careful consistency of the rest of the family. A child will accept, without question, fair and consistent rules and regulations. He will obey them and learn to be a cooperative member of the family, if he is not confused and upset by zigzags in the way he is treated by different people in his home environment.

Beliefs to hold on to

8. *Have strong but tolerant beliefs regarding the important things of life, and let your child know that there are certain things he must learn to accept and believe.* A too-critical attitude toward religion, law, relatives, or other people will give a child a feeling of insecurity because it gives him nothing positive to stand on to gain a firm footing. In place of such attitudes, give your child beliefs that he can accept. These will give him the basis for firm convictions as he grows older and is capable of thinking for himself.

Inferiority complex

When a child has an inferiority complex, does it mean that he feels insecure? Our Tommy, who is 7 years old, has an inferiority complex, his teacher tells us.

I RATHER question whether a 7-year-old has an "inferiority complex," though it would be well to heed his teacher's warning and find out what is back of it. Every inferiority complex is built up on a person's strong feeling of *inadequacy.* Back of this feeling of inadequacy is a feeling of *insecurity* which stems from uncertainty as to how the individual stands in different environments and as to how people feel about him.

To keep your Tommy from developing a real inferiority complex, you will do well to find out what lies back of his feeling of insecurity. This you can discover by listening carefully to what he says about himself, his relationships with the family and his friends, and his abilities. If, for example, he says, "I can't play ball as well as the other fellows" or "I can't do arithmetic" or "Johnny is lucky because his family has a car and a television set and we don't," then you know where his feeling of inadequacy comes from.

If he feels insecure at home, in school, or among his playmates, it will then be up to you to try to build up in the child feelings of security to replace his present feelings of insecurity. Don't make the mistake of believing that this change will come about of its own accord as the child grows older and has wider experiences. The chances are that the opposite will happen.

Moral standards

We have very strict standards of right and wrong at home. My daughter, Gail, is in the third grade and is beginning to tell us that we are too "strict." From what she tells us, her friends' parents allow their children to do many things we would never allow Gail to do. How will this affect her?

CHANCES are that the difference between your standards and those of Gail's friends will so confuse the child that it will give her a feeling of insecurity about what is right and what is wrong. Why not discuss with some of her friends' parents this matter of what they allow their children to do? Children sometimes do a lot of exaggerating and Gail may be getting a false picture of what her friends are permitted to do.

After finding out what the other children are allowed to do, you may find it wise to revalue your own standards to see if they are too strict. You do not want to penalize Gail by requiring her to do things the other children are not expected to do. Likely they do nothing wrong even if their rules are more lenient than yours.

Moving from place to place

My husband's business requires us to move from place to place. While our two children were babies, it didn't matter much, but now that they are both of school age, I am worried about what effect this constant moving will have on the children.

IT IS, of course, much better for children to grow up in a place where they can get their roots into the ground. However, this is not always possible. As your husband's work requires moving, you must make the best possible adjustment to the situation. As soon as you get into a new place, make an effort to establish yourself through the church, the school your children attend, and through different community organizations. This will help your children too.

Keep open house for your children's classmates and make special efforts to entertain their friends. See that your children wear the same clothes, have much the same playthings, and are governed by the same rules as their classmates. If you find they lack some play skill in vogue in the new community, employ a high school student to help your children to learn this skill. So long as children are much the same in looks and behavior as the other children, it does not take long for them to find a place for themselves in their community. And, once they find that place, there will be no reason for them to feel insecure or out of things.

Living with sister

I am a widow and must work to support myself and my 4-year-old son. I have a room in my sister's home and she takes care of my son while I work. I do not feel that this is the way to bring up a child but what can I do?

You are doubtless doing the best you can under the circumstances. At least, your son has the stability of a home and an aunt to take care of him while you are at work. The important thing for the child is for you and your sister to agree upon discipline for the child so that you will not contradict each other in what he is permitted to do when he is with either one of you.

It would be far better for your son if you could find someone you loved enough to marry. Then your son would have a home of his own, you could stay at home with him, and he would have a father to replace the one he has lost. Ideally, you should remarry as soon as possible so as to provide the permanence in your son's life that is not possible under your present living conditions.

Financial matters

Is it wise to discuss financial matters before children?

How you discuss the financial matters is more important than anything else. If you approach such matters in a calm, unemotional manner, your children will accept them in a like manner and will not be upset by them. You can say, for example, "I wish we could buy a television set but it is very expensive and we need a new refrigerator more. Maybe next year we can buy the television set." This will not upset the child nor will it give him a feeling of insecurity about the family's financial status.

But if you complain about not having enough money to buy what other people have and let the child know that you feel like a martyr as a result, it will foster a feeling of insecurity about how the family stands financially. Continual grumblings of this sort on the part of his parents will, eventually, wear away the child's feeling of security in this area of his life. This, in turn, may readily spread to other areas of his life, thus leading to a general feeling of insecurity.

Financial uncertainty

My husband gets tired of work and always loses jobs. While he works, we manage to get along. Then, when he is out of work, I often have to take a job to pay for our rent and food. I feel this is very bad for the whole family but the children are the real sufferers.

Y<small>OU</small> are right. Your children *are* the real sufferers in this up-and-down sort of life you are leading. Surely your husband must realize that it is his responsibility to provide for his family and, in fairness to you and the children, he cannot let his boredom with a job influence his work to the point where he loses his job.

To provide some stability in the family's life, why not urge him to have some vocational tests to find out what sort of work he is best fitted for and what sort he would enjoy doing? If he could settle down to a line of work he liked and could do well, it would not only supply the family with the stability it now lacks but it might even lead to promotions, from which the whole family would benefit. Even without the promotions, there would be some steadiness in your life which is now lacking.

Husband in service

My husband is in the service and will be away for three years. We own our home and, with careful management, I can keep the home while he is away. My parents think I should take the two children and live where my husband is stationed. Would you advise this?

I<small>F YOU</small> could be certain that your husband would be stationed at only one place during his three years of service and that he would not be sent overseas, it would be better to keep the family together by moving to where he is stationed. However, because this is unlikely, it would be better for you and your husband to make the personal sacrifice of being separated so you can keep your children in the stability of their own home while he is away. If he is near enough, he could come home on leave from time to time and you and the children could go to visit him. But, having a place they can return to and that they can call "home" is very important to children, especially when they are old enough to go to school and to have friends outside the home.

chapter 26

Every child
needs to achieve

ONLY when a child has reasonable success in what he undertakes can he develop self-confidence. And only when he has this self-confidence can he tackle problems as they arise and be willing to work hard to achieve new successes. His *Success leads* success in a few areas of life, like sports and school, quickly *to success* spreads to other areas, like getting along with others. In time, the child develops a "success complex"—the feeling that he can meet tasks successfully.

Without success, he can't develop self-confidence. And without self-confidence, he soon develops feelings of insecurity. These weaken his desire to tackle problems and tasks which he could do as well as any other child *if* he had confidence in his abilities to meet them successfully.

Failures, especially if they are severe and if they come often, pave the way for feelings of inferiority, for a "failure *Failures* complex." Once this is developed, the child is not only un- *breed failure* happy but is doomed to failure in whatever he undertakes throughout his life. Failures in childhood are serious, therefore, and should be carefully guarded against.

Success complex or failure complex—which will your child develop? It will depend, to a large extent, upon you and upon the way you guide him during the long and difficult years of establishing himself in his world.

Few children succeed in what they attempt without the help and guidance, along with careful planning, of their parents, teachers, older relatives and friends. True, children may work hard and conscientiously to achieve their goal—but their lack of knowledge and their inexperience doom them to failure. Not knowing how to do the task, they use a hit-or-miss approach, and the chances of failure are far greater than the chances of success.

Guidance along the road to success

There is much a parent can do, therefore, to help the child achieve *what he is capable of* and at the age when he is capable of success in that particular task. By his success, the child develops confidence in his abilities, a quality essential to a happy, useful life.

Since success is essential to the building of self-confidence, should a child be spared all failures? No; on the contrary: failures, if not too severe or too frequent, are essential if a child is to learn to size up his abilities.

Some failure can give balance

You have probably known a child who, through mistaken kindness on the part of his parents, *always* succeeds in whatever he undertakes because of the help given by his parents. Such a child soon develops a cocky attitude about what he can do, and, in time, tries to step where angels fear to tread. If he isn't helped out of his predicament, he will get into such trouble that he won't be able to get out without burning his fingers.

A few well-controlled failures, on the other hand, are as essential to a child as success. Without these failures, he cannot estimate his abilities correctly, nor develop a down-to-earth attitude toward his own abilities. But, like success, failures cannot be left to chance. It is the parent's responsibility to see to it that the child has the right number of failures and of suitable severity.

But failure needs to be controlled

I think Tommy's case illustrates this point. Tommy, age 7, wants to play baseball because he sees the older boys playing this game and he thinks it would be more fun than the simpler ball games his age group plays. Should his father encourage him to try to play baseball just because Tommy wants to do so? Yes—if Tommy has shown a real ability to throw, catch, and hit balls with a bat. But if Tommy is all thumbs when he tries to catch a ball, how can he possibly learn to play baseball until he has acquired the foundation skills for this game? And he can't learn these skills just by *wanting* to do so. He will need months or perhaps even years of practice to lay the foundations for the complicated skills he will need to play baseball with the older boys.

What Tommy's father can do

Tommy's father should not encourage him to take up baseball just because Tommy wants to do so. Yet he should not discourage him by flatly telling him he can't play ball games well enough. Father should show Tommy why he is not yet ready for baseball by showing him what skills are needed, how long it takes one to learn such skills, and by emphasizing the fact that most boys cannot play this game until they are years older than Tommy. A demonstration with a ball and bat will show Tommy what his father means. This kind of *controlled* failure will not build up a feeling of defeat in Tommy but will give him the necessary push to practice until he is ready to learn to play baseball.

Helping children to achieve success

Since few children can achieve success by themselves, parents ought to guide their children so that successes are guaranteed in sufficient numbers to develop the self-confidence a child needs to achieve successes for himself as he grows older. These are some of the things parents can do:

Keeping the child's feet on the ground

1. *Help your child to set practical goals for himself.* Let him know whether he has the necessary abilities or experience to succeed in whatever he undertakes, or whether he is aiming at a goal way beyond his *present* capacities. This should be done with great tact and understanding to avoid giving the child the feeling that you doubt his ability. Explain why he is not ready at this time to do what he wants to do and encourage him by telling him at about what age the things he wants to do can be done successfully. Don't tell him he can do whatever he wants to so long as he is willing to try. Trying is *not* enough! Every child, because of his limited knowledge and experience, has an urge to reach for the moon and touch it.

Then he is bitterly disappointed when he fails to do so. That is why it is important for parents to help the child estimate his abilities realistically and to set goals for himself that he can reach successfully. This way he won't doubt his own abilities and decide he is a failure.

2. *Show your child how to achieve the goals he sets for himself by teaching him the best and most efficient methods to use.* Left to his own devices, he would, in time and with great effort, achieve fair success, if the goals were within his reach. But inefficient methods take too much of the child's time and energy; they bring discouragement and a feeling of inadequacy.

Help him learn good methods

3. *Be ready to advise and help when your child hits a snag.* Because he is still young and inexperienced, you cannot expect him to know how to overcome obstacles alone. A few words of advice from you, or a helping hand when he needs it, may be all that is necessary to turn failure into success. But wait until you see the child really needs your help before offering it. Otherwise you are likely to make him dependent upon you to the point where he will doubt his own abilities.

Know when to lend a hand

4. *Guide your child's activities within the range of his abilities.* You can tell, from the way he attacks a task, whether he can make a success of it or not. This does not mean that you should keep him down to a level where achievement will be so easy that he needs to put forth little effort. On the contrary, be sure that some of the tasks he tackles are difficult enough to tax his capacities and thus give him an incentive to strive hard. Success won in a difficult task does far more to build up a child's self-confidence than success won when the task has been so easy for him that it required little effort.

Tasks should not be too easy

5. *Don't let your child's achievements become one-sided.* If he is to feel self-confidence, he must have reasonable successes in the majority of things he tries to do. Marked success in a few activities accomplished by failures or near-failures in other activities will not be enough to establish a success attitude in a child. Only after a child has learned to do with reasonable success the many things he wants to do and that the other children do, should he begin to specialize.

6. *Plan your child's daily schedule so that he has at least one achievement each day that he can feel proud of.* Boost his pride in his achievement by praising him for it. A real achievement, especially if won by his own hard and persistent effort, will do much to lessen the discouragement that is bound to

At least one success a day

come from any failures the child may have. If he has a success as the day comes to an end, he can go to bed with the thought, "I did this very well today." He will waken the next morning with the eagerness necessary to start the new day confident that he can make as great a success of it as he did of the days that are already past.

Achievements should be balanced

W<small>E HAVE</small> already seen that it isn't enough for a child to be successful in *one* area of his life and feel inadequate in others. The failures he meets in his daily living when his achievements in different tasks fall below his hopes will have a piling-up effect. They give him the impression that he is a failure. Even outstanding achievements in one or two areas will not make up for these failures.

I don't mean that we can expect any child to be equally succes.ful in everything he undertakes. No matter how hard he may strive for success, he may be limited by his own inborn capacity for that particular kind of activity. However, we can *A reasonable approach* help him to make a reasonable success of whatever he undertakes. And if the tasks he tackles are within his ability to handle successfully, he is well on the way toward developing a confident attitude that he *can* do what he sets out to do.

An illustration will help to show the importance of this approach to the building of self-confidence in children. For a 9-year-old, Johnny Green is a talented pianist. Certainly he far *An example of one-sidedness* surpasses any of his classmates in this achievement. But he has gained his skill at the piano by sacrificing other areas of his development. At games and sports he is all thumbs, with the result that the other boys do not want to include him in their play. Because he has so few opportunities to show off his musical skill, Johnny feels that he is a failure when he compares himself with his classmates.

Similarly, Mary Norval has been trained to be a helpmate to her mother in the home. Even though she is only 8, Mary *Another example of lack of balance* can sew her own clothes with help from her mother, prepare a simple meal for the family, and take charge of the younger children while her mother is out of the house. These domestic skills have been learned at the expense of skills useful in playing with others her age. So long as she is at home, Mary's achievements give her plenty of self-confidence and self-assurance. But in school, or on the playground, Mary is in much the same position as Johnny Green: her lack of achievement in play makes her feel inadequate. The result is that she shuns play with children and spends most of her out-of-school time within the walls of her home where her achievements give her poise and self-confidence.

Four areas in which children should achieve

HERE are some of the areas of life in which an American child of today should achieve reasonable success if he or she is to build up a poised and self-confident personality:

1. *Physical Achievements.* Because play is so important in the life of a child, he must be able to play as well as, if not slightly better than, others his age if he is to feel secure. Lack of achievement in this area is very serious because it cuts the child off from contacts with children at the age when such contacts are essential to his happiness.

Control of his body

The child of today must be able to do most of the things for himself that are essential to independence. This means self-dressing, self-bathing, self-feeding, going places in the neighborhood alone, and being able to handle his toys without help from adults. By the time a child reaches the kindergarten age and spends much of his waking time with other children in school or in the neighborhood, he feels very inadequate if his achievement along these lines falls below that of his playmates.

2. *Intellectual Achievements.* A child whose school grades are below those of his classmates or his intimate friends is likely to feel very inadequate. Because of his lack of success, he may dislike school and use every possible opportunity to avoid going to school. The situation is made worse when his parents show an unsympathetic attitude toward his lack of achievement in school and treat his failures as if they were due to lack of effort on his part.

Good use of his mental ability

But this area of achievement is not limited to getting good grades in school. Intellectual achievements also include ability to read, to do simple puzzles and guessing games, and to count well enough to play games requiring scores or to go to the store on errands for mother. The child whose capacity is below average soon discovers his shortcomings both in and out of school. He always compares what *he* can do with what other children can do, and this quickly makes him feel inferior.

Feelings of inferiority

Fortunately for children who are not bright, schools of today often group together children whose intellectual capacities are approximately equal. As a result, both in school and in play, the not-too-bright child is spared the constant reminder of his lack of ability along these lines. He can compare his achievements with those of children whose abilities are similar to his, not with those whose inborn intelligence makes their achievements superior to his.

3. *Moral Achievements.* Doing what is right—that's a feather in any child's cap! Being praised or rewarded for this achievement doubles the pleasure a child gets out of it, and makes him want to continue to do the right things. On the surface, a naughty child may seem to be getting pleasure from the trouble and annoyance he causes others. But he isn't, actually. He's being naughty because he is not receiving the recognition he craves for his achievements in other areas of his life. He is trying to offset this by using the only method he has found that will give him at least temporary satisfaction.

There's joy in doing what is right

To achieve socially approved behavior is extremely important to a child's social adjustments and to a favorable idea of himself as an individual. That is why it is important for parents to teach the child the right way to behave and encourage him, by praise for his achievements, to behave in a manner that will guarantee the social approval that is essential to happiness and feelings of self-assurance. Discipline, carefully planned and carried out, is thus essential not only to good behavior but also to the building up of a personality pattern that will lead to future happiness when parents are not available to guide the child's behavior.

Sensible discipline is valuable

4. *Spiritual Achievements.* No matter how young the child, he must have faith in something greater than all of us. This faith is supplied by his religious teachings. To enable the child to derive the satisfaction that comes from the spiritual area of his life, the religious teachings should not be of the narrow, dogmatic type. Instead, I think they should include a broad, unprejudiced outlook on life, a "philosophy of life" which will guide his behavior and enable him to feel that he knows where life is leading him and what he wants to achieve from life. Belief in ideals, loyalty to friends and country, and love for the beautiful—all add to his feeling of belonging. They are essential to the self-assurance which far too few children achieve.

Achieving a faith in life

Disappointments

My son feels that he can do anything and is not willing to take advice. When he does not succeed in what he undertakes, he is disappointed and discouraged. He is only 8 years old and I tell him he can't expect to do new things without help.

Most 8-year-olds have a cocky self-confidence that makes giving them advice almost impossible. To some extent, your son will have to learn through his failures what he can and cannot do. However, it isn't wise to allow a child to learn too much in that way because repeated failures and disappointments are likely to build up in him a feeling of inadequacy.

You might be able to help your son to judge his abilities and disabilities more accurately if you explain to him what different tasks require in the way of skill and experience. For example: he may say, "Anyone can fix a broken television set." Without suggesting that you doubt his ability to fix the set, tell him about the training and experience necessary to fix broken electrical appliances. He will then realize that there actually *are* some things he cannot do.

Too much success

I have always heard that too much success turns a person's head and makes him lazy and conceited. Should a child be permitted to be too successful?

Too much of anything is bad for anyone, whether it be too much success, too much money, or too much rich food. When a person has an excess of anything, he loses his sense of values and gets the wrong slant on things. That is why he needs some bad to offset too much good.

Repeated successes without occasional failures are likely to give a child a false idea of his abilities. Then, when he hits a snag, his pride is hurt and he cannot understand what is the matter. Instead of recognizing *he* is at fault, he is likely to lay the blame for the failure on someone else. This certainly is not going to help him to make good adjustments to life, nor will it enable him to know what he can and cannot do.

Children are more likely to have too many failures than too many successes. If a child does have too many successes, it's because he is kept from attempting things he might be unable to do, or because he gets so much help from others that his triumphs are only partly his. So, if you find that your child is meeting too few setbacks, and if you have reason to believe that he is therefore developing a distorted idea of his abilities, find out what is responsible for all these successes. Are you helping him too much? Are you holding him back from trying things he might not be able to do? If the blame is with you, change your methods. Let your child have an occasional taste of failure to balance his surplus of successes.

Pride in achievement

I have noticed that all of my children get tremendous pleasure from doing things well, even if it means hard work. I think too many parents of young children today are prone to make life too easy for their children's good.

You are absolutely correct about this. Far too many parents make life much too easy for their children. They are so anxious to make childhood a pleasant period that they take away from youngsters one of the greatest sources of happiness any child can have—the pleasure that comes from being able to do things for himself. Besides depriving a child of this very important source of happiness, parents make the child dependent upon someone's help, thus killing the child's self-confidence. The lack of self-confidence that comes from over-dependency in the childhood years will pave the way for unhappiness in later years.

Self-confidence

The teacher tells us that our son, Ronnie, who is in the third grade, could do good work if he only had more self-confidence. We have noticed at home that he seems to be afraid to try anything new without help from us. What makes a child lack self-confidence and what can a parent do to build it up?

First, I must say that you, as parents, are partly if not wholly to blame for Ronnie's situation. Without meaning to do so, I am sure, you have doubtless expected more of Ronnie than he was capable of, you have criticized his achievements because they did not come up to your expectations, or you have compared him unfavorably with other children in the home or neighborhood. Have you really given him much praise or shown real pride in his achievements? I doubt it—or the boy would not be so lacking in self-confidence.

Building up self-confidence is much harder than tearing it down. But you must do all you can to make Ronnie reasonably confident of his abilities. You can do this by using praise in place of criticism. If he needs to be criticized, be sure to do it in a positive way, combined with praise to remove the sting that comes with direct criticism. Tell Ronnie, for example: "You did a good job of raking the leaves. I appreciate all the work you put into fixing up the lawn." Then, as if an afterthought, suggest that the lawn would look even better if he would pull the dead leaves out from under the bushes by hand instead of leaving them there or breaking some of the branches of the bushes by trying to rake under them. Criticism given this way will have no sting to it, and may not even be recognized by the child as criticism.

Another thing you can do for Ronnie's self-confidence is to control his activities so that his successes will overshadow his failures. See to it that he does not attempt to do things you know he cannot do, and help him when he needs your help to finish what he tackles. In time, he will realize from his achievements that he is not lacking in ability as he once thought he was. This realization will gradually increase his self-confidence.

Cheating

Our children have been brought up to believe that cheating is wrong and, so far as I know, they do not cheat. But they are getting very discouraged because they get poorer grades than some who study much less but copy other children's work. How can I convince my children that they are better off with poorer grades, honestly won?

You are expecting your children to have a very mature outlook on life if you expect them to be satisfied with honestly earned grades that fall below those won with the least effort or with dishonesty. However, you must try to make them realize that "crime never pays" and that the cheaters will, sooner or later, pay the price of dishonesty when they are caught, as cheaters always are.

As long as you show that *you* are perfectly satisfied with their grades, when they are won honestly, your children will have less reason to follow the lead of those who cheat. Many children develop into cheaters not because of laziness, but rather because the work they are capable of doing is not good enough to satisfy their parents. This gives the child a motive to cheat so he can bring home good grades and thus win parental approval.

Understanding prayer

We are having a difficult problem with our 8-year-old daughter. She has said her prayers faithfully ever since she was old enough to talk. Now she claims it does no good to pray as God never gives you what you ask for. How can we answer her arguments?

If you have taught your daughter that prayer is a way of getting things you want just by asking for them, you must change your teaching so your daughter will get a different idea of the meaning of prayer. She must learn that achievement comes only through effort by the person; just *asking* is not enough. Many children, unfortunately, grow up with the same sort of doubt your daughter is now experiencing. As a result, they begin to question if there is anything in religion for them. I suggest that you have the minister of your church, or your daughter's Sunday school teacher, talk over this matter with her and try to straighten out her notion of the meaning of prayer.

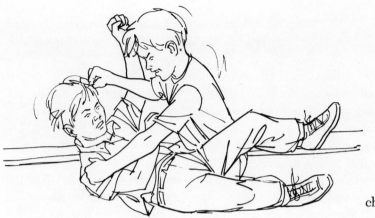

chapter 27

Everyday
problems

Temper tantrums—shyness—lying—stubbornness—whining—
these are a few of the common "problem behaviors" I want
to discuss in this chapter.

They are some of the many, many things every child
does, at some time or other, which disturb his parents and are
labeled "problem behavior." But some things are so universal
that we may almost consider them "normal." These are the
behaviors that belong to certain stages of growing up. Very
often they are a result of the child's ignorance *and* the parent's
bungling.

Handled wisely, these habits will be put away with other
childish things as the child moves into a more mature stage
of his development. Handled poorly, however, they may become real problems. They can often develop into behavior
patterns that bring grief to parents and failure to the child.

How do *you* handle a situation where your child's behavior does not come up to accepted standards? What *should*
parents do about these everyday situations? How *can* we avoid
making mistakes when things like these happen—

Some "problems"
are part of
growing up

Wise handling
forestalls real
problems

Temper tantrums

What can I do to stop my 4-year-old's temper tantrums?
He goes into such fits that he wears himself out.

Your child is now at the peak of the temper tantrum age. Each month, from now on, you should find a gradual decline in the number and severity of his tantrums. However, you can hasten this decline by tactful handling of the situation. Give him warning of what you will ask him to do, instead of springing it on him. Try to divert his attention to something pleasant when you see he is getting tense. Give him reasons that he can understand for what you ask him to do. And—above all—*keep calm yourself* when you see he is getting ready for a tantrum. While the tantrum is on, leave the room—don't try to argue with him. After he has cooled down, you can talk the matter over with him and get him to see how foolish his tantrums are.

Alibis

What do you do with a child who always has an alibi
for something he did that was wrong?

Show him it is poor sportsmanship to try to blame someone else for his own faults. Then, don't criticize or punish him when he frankly admits that he was at fault. Making alibis is a defense for feelings of being inadequate built up from too much criticism or punishment. Of course, you will point out to your child why he was wrong at times, and you will punish when necessary. But first make sure that his misdeeds were intentional and not due to ignorance or inexperience.

Stealing

My son, age 7, takes things from other children and
has even taken money from my pocketbook.
I am worried because I feel Sam is too old for this.

Are you sure Sam understands how wrong it is to take something from anyone without first asking permission? Many parents make the mistake of taking for granted that the child knows it is wrong to do this. As a result, they never really explain to him why he should not take things. Perhaps your son feels that family property is community property, and that it is quite all right to use other people's things.

Ask Sam to come to you when there is something he wants very much, and to ask you for it. If reasonable and possible, you will give it to him. When a child feels confident that his parents will grant him his requests, if possible, he is less likely to have the urge to take things. If, after a reasonable time, these suggestions do not bring results, consult a child guidance specialist to find out what is back of your child's stealing.

Excessive shyness

My daughter is overly shy. She will enter first grade next fall,
and I am afraid she will be very unhappy in school.
What can I do to help her?

AT YOUR daughter's age, excessive shyness is usually a result of a too restricted life, with too few opportunities for contact with people. It may also come from unpleasant experiences with people outside the home. Try having one or two children of her age over to your home to play with her. Stay around until you feel she is at ease with them. Encourage her to play with the neighbors' children. Take her shopping with you or calling on your friends, and have her stay around when you have company. If possible, send her to a kindergarten; it will help her feel at ease in school.

If there are any signs that she actually dreads meeting and being with people, try to get her to tell you what is back of her dread. Usually contacts with people day in and day out will cure a child of excessive shyness.

No initiative

What do you do with a child who shows no initiative
and who depends on someone to do everything for him?
I even have to tell my 7-year-old boy what to play!

WHEN a child lacks initiative, his *parents* are usually to blame. They have done too much of his thinking for him, and he has developed the habit of depending on them.

Stop doing your son's thinking for him. Let *him* shoulder that responsibility. Even if he is late for school, misses a meal, or sits around with nothing to do—let *him* find his own way out. Give him help only when he has tried and failed. He will learn, in time, that he must stand on his own feet, that he must make his own mistakes just as other people do. It may take time to create this desire to do things for himself—but it will take less time now than if you wait until he is older.

Standing up for rights

My children all seem to allow other children to take advantage of them.
Is this the fault of my training?

IF YOU have forbidden your children to fight for their rights and have punished them when they did, you cannot blame them now for not showing righteous indignation. Explain to them that there is a big difference between starting a fight and fighting when attacked. Encourage them to fight back—either with words or with fists—when others take advantage of them. When the other children discover that your children aren't easy marks, your children will seldom have to use their fists.

Disorderliness

My three children are ages 3 to 10. They are the most disorderly
children I have ever seen, really. I don't understand it because
I have always prided myself on being neat as a pin.

ARE you assuming that your children would inherit your quality of being "neat as a pin"? Or are you actually training them to be neat and orderly with their appearance and their possessions? Don't count on nature doing *your* job. Orderliness is not an inherited trait. It must be taught—and it takes a long time to learn it.

Don't expect your children to develop into orderly people overnight, even if you work hard to train them. If they make *some* improvement from month to month, be satisfied. Work with them to establish efficient ways of keeping things in order. Provide ample places for them to keep their things. Then reward them when they do a good job. By the time they reach your age, they, too, may be "neat as pins"—but don't be disappointed if they are not. Excessive orderliness is not essential to happiness, though it is true that you can live more comfortably and work more efficiently if you are reasonably orderly.

Selfishness

My son, who is just 5, is very selfish about his toys. This is
making him unpopular with the other children.
And he always fights if his younger brother touches
anything of his. How can I make him less selfish?

FIRST—and most important—you must curb the jealousy that lies behind your son's selfishness. He feels insecure in your love, and clings to his possessions as a source of security. Naturally, the traits he shows at home carry over to his contacts outside the home. This selfishness will make him more and more unpopular as he grows older and finds the other children sharing better with playmates than he does.

Encourage the baby brother to share with him and have your 5-year-old share with the baby. You and your husband must share your things with your son, too, so he will realize this is the way to treat everyone. When anything of his is broken or damaged, get him a new one to replace it. And when he shows willingness to share, reward him by praise. At 5, all children are somewhat selfish. But it must be corrected before it settles into a habit.

Too generous

What do you do with a child who is too generous? My 7-year-old daughter would give the shirt off her back if I would let her.

OVER-GENEROSITY, like selfishness, shows poor adjustment. Your daughter is literally "buying popularity" by giving away her things to others who admire them or who show some interest in them. This kind of bribery never wins friends in the long run; your child will feel bitterly crushed when she discovers this. Try to convince her that she should not try to win favor with others by giving them her things, for people seldom appreciate what is dropped into their laps. And they don't respect the person who does the dropping.

Let her exchange things for something which another child has and she wants, and encourage her to share her things with others. But insist that they be returned and that she ask your permission before giving away anything of hers. This will give you good opportunities to discuss the matter with her whenever the occasion arises, and to point out to her why she should, or should not, give that particular thing to that particular person. Be careful, however, that your training does not swing her into the opposite direction of selfishness.

Daydreaming

My son is a daydreamer. David is in second grade and does very poor work because he just does not pay attention. At home he sits around looking off into space, instead of playing with the children. What is wrong with him?

IT IS perfectly normal for children to daydream to some extent, especially when they are bored or unhappy. But David's daydreaming is going beyond reasonable limits. It points to poor adjustments on his part. If the cause cannot be found and corrected, he will spend more and more time in his daydream world, and will make poorer and poorer adjustments to life. I urge you to see a child guidance specialist to find out why your son is retreating from reality into the happier world of daydreams. Clearly, he is unhappy about something—otherwise why does he feel the need to escape from the life around him?

Tattle tale

What is the best way of handling tattling? My older daughter, who is 9, is always tattling on her younger sister and brother.

Don't listen to the tales she brings to you. Tell your daughter it is not fair to her brother and sister to talk about them behind their backs. Then try to make her feel that you love her as much as you love the other two children. Tattling is a bid for attention. Children usually do it if they feel they are neglected or don't get the attention other children receive. When you can correct this notion, your daughter will have little reason to tattle on her brother and sister.

Whiner

My daughter is just 5. When she cannot have her way, she whines and cries until it finally gets on my nerves and I give in to her. I know this is wrong because she whines so much that her voice has a whining tone even when she is cheerful. How can I correct this?

You must first correct your own sensitivity to her whines. Don't let her see that her whining gets on your nerves. Go out of the room if necessary, but don't give in unless you see that she is right. Suggest that she smile when she talks as it will make her voice "sound better." Children's voices are easily changed. It should not take long to get the whine out of your daughter's voice if you see to it that she stops the whining when she cannot get what she wants. The firmer you are, the sooner you will correct this habit she is slipping into.

Whoppers

My boy, who is just 7 years old, tells such whoppers that I am surprised that he can think anyone would believe him. How can I get him to stop?

Are you sure your son is even conscious that what he says is obviously untrue? It sounds to me like a case of vivid imagination without a reasoning ability that is mature enough to keep it within bounds. To help him develop this essential brake on his vivid imagination, question him—kindly but pointedly—about the things he tells you. Don't ridicule him or accuse him of lying, but lead him on to see how absurd some of his statements are. Then ask if he is telling a true story or a pretend story. Tell him it is fun to make up a pretend story, but when he wants people to believe him, he must tell a true story. If you do this consistently, he will gradually learn to distinguish between fact and fantasy and to understand when he may use imagination and when he must tell the exact truth.

Stubbornness

I realize that determination is a good quality, while stubbornness just for the sake of having your own way is bad. My daughter Elsie is of the second type. How can I turn her stubbornness into determination?

You can do this best by helping Elsie to develop a better sense of values than most children have. Her determination to have her own way, right or wrong, and to persist in what she is doing, whether she is on the right track or not, will certainly get her into trouble sooner or later. Let her burn her fingers and stub her toes once in a while. Then, after the hurt has gone, try to show her that she can blame no one but herself. In time she will realize that she does not know all there is to know. She will be more willing to listen to reason or to seek advice. When this happens, her pigheadedness will develop into the kind of determination that will be a plus rather than a minus for her.

Sulkiness

What can a mother do to a child who sulks every time he is told he cannot do or have what he wants? My son used to be a crybaby. Now that he is in second grade, he has stopped crying but he sulks instead. This bothers me as I feel it will make him very unpopular.

You are right: sulkiness does not help children make friends. Their classmates take it as poor sportsmanship—and no one likes a poor sport. There are two things you can do; one negative, the other positive. The negative approach is to pay no attention to your son when he sulks, and never to give in to him in this mood. In time he will discover that sulking does not work.

On the positive side, try to explain to him how other people re-act to his sulkiness. Would he want to be friends with a boy who sulked when he could not get his own way? Choose a time when he is in good spirits for this discussion. You cannot reason with him when he is in a sulky mood.

Boasting

One of my son's kindergarten playmates is always boasting about the things he has. His parents are well-to-do and, as he is an only child, they shower him with things most of us just cannot afford. My boy and the other children feel abused. What can I do about it?

FIRST: Your son's playmate boasts because he feels insecure and he is bidding for attention in this way. He does not realize how it affects the other children. SECOND: You cannot blame your child for being envious. He is too young to realize that material possessions are not essential to happiness. He merely wants—as all children want—things that a boaster has glamorized.

Why not discuss the problem with the kindergarten teacher and let her handle it with the child or with his parents? I'm sure she must realize that the boasting does not give the child the popularity he craves, and that it is bad for the group's morale. If she cannot make headway with the child himself, she can urge his parents to limit their gifts to what the other children have. She can urge them to encourage their child to be generous in sharing what he has with the children who have less. Each year, as this boy grows older, his boasting will make him less and less popular. Now is the ideal time to nip it in the bud. Perhaps his parents do not realize this.

Tact

I have noticed that children say very cruel, tactless things— not only to each other but also to older people. How can a parent cultivate tact in a child?

CULTIVATING tact is a long, slow, hard process. There must first be a level of mental maturity that comes with the growth of intelligence and from many, varied experiences with people. To a certain extent, however, you *can* speed up this process. Try to point out to the child how *he* would feel if *he* were in the shoes of someone who was spoken to rudely or unkindly, or whose feelings had been hurt by thoughtless people. Whenever you hear your child make an untactful remark, explain how he was hurting the other person by what he said. In time he will realize the sting in such remarks. And this will be the beginning of his growth in tact.

Vivid imagination

My 6-year-old daughter has a very vivid imagination. Dot loves fairy tales and is always dressing up and pretending she is someone else. Won't this turn into daydreaming? It already makes her tell many things that are not true. How can I curb Dot's imagination?

I F I were you, I would not "curb" your child's imagination. Instead, cultivate it. Encourage Dot to turn it into more useful channels. Her imagination can be a great asset to her in life if it is harnessed and used for practical purposes instead of being allowed to run wild. Encourage some listening to realistic stories instead of a diet too heavy in fairy tales. At play time, insist that she play games with the girls and boys of the neighborhood instead of dressing up. Also, show her the exaggerations in the things she says. Dot is now at the peak of the growth of her imagination. In a few years, her reasoning ability will catch up and will then act as a *natural* curb on her too vivid imagination.

Shiftiness

My daughter never gives me a straight answer. She always beats around the bush and tries to change the subject when I reprove her for something. I hate sneakiness in children, and I want to correct it before it becomes a habit.

A CHILD is evasive because he is afraid of possible punishment if he tells the truth. Make your little girl see that not giving a straight answer is a sign that she knows she was wrong, and that she will be punished for it. At the same time, tell her that you will not punish her if she tells the truth in a straightforward manner—no matter how wrong the act may be. You must then live up to your word if you want her to get over the habit of evading the truth. I think you are very wise to try to break up this tendency before it settles into a firm habit. By that time it might be too late to change it.

Brash and forward

I have noticed that since my daughter started school in September, she is very "fresh" and forward. She used to be a very quiet, respectful child. I don't like this change in her, and yet I don't quite know how to correct it.

W ITHIN limits, your daughter is going through a phase that is very typical for her age. Most children show this revolt against adult authority when they are old enough to go to school. The *extent* of her change is partly *your* fault. You encouraged her to be "too good" for her age, when she was younger. Now she is rebelling more violently than she would if she had not been such a quiet, respectful little girl.

Let her get some of this revolt out of her system without saying much about it. When she realizes that you are not trying to crush her, she will be more willing to listen to reason when you explain that she is being very rude and that it will make people dislike her. It is better for a child to be a bit too forward than too quiet and suppressed. Brashness can be checked in time, but the other becomes more and more deeply rooted with advancing years.

Suspiciousness

No matter what we say or do, our son is suspicious of our motives. He is the same way with the other children in school and with his teachers. Why doesn't he trust people?

Your son must have had experiences that disappointed him and made him lose faith in people. Until you can restore that faith in people—in his parents, schoolmates, and teachers in particular—he will continue to be suspicious.

At home you can do a lot to rebuild his faith in others by being very careful to do whatever you say you will do, by explaining to him fully why you do or say what you do, and by giving him clear reasons for any punishment you must give him. Encourage him to *talk* about his suspicions so you can see if they are justified. You can help him gain a healthier outlook by talking over matters that lead up to his suspicions.

chapter 28

How do I rate
as a parent?

*Do your children love and respect you—or do they think
you are cross and unreasonable?*

*Do they think you are fair—or do they accuse you of being
"mean" and playing favorites?*

*Do they respect your judgment and feel you are fair,
though strict, in your discipline—or do they consider you an
"easy mark"?*

THESE are some of the questions you, as a parent, will do
well to ask yourself. Gone are the days of "Mother knows best,"
of father as almighty ruler of the home. At home or school,
children today are encouraged to think for themselves, to express opinions frankly. So parents are no exception: they, too,
come under the child's critical eye.

*Times have
changed*

How your children feel about you *as a person* and *as a
parent* is vitally important to them, to you, and to the happiness of the whole family. No, it isn't enough for your children
to like you as a person, but not respect you as a parent. And it

isn't enough for them to think you make a good parent, if, at the same time, they don't have the same emotional warmth for you that they have for others outside the family circle.

How children judge parents

THE way a child judges his parents depends partly on the standards his parents use in judging people, and partly on the standards his friends use in judging others. If parents or friends take an overly critical attitude, the child will imitate it; his judgments of his parents will be harsh and intolerant. If parents and friends are tolerant, the child, too, can develop a more understanding attitude toward others.

When children criticize

After a child begins to play with other children, he will hear from these children how they feel about their parents. Most children are outspoken in their criticism of the things their parents do which they dislike. So a child who used to take what his parents did or said in a matter-of-fact way, will now openly criticize them if he is not reproved or punished for this. His outspoken accusations will likely become stronger and more frequent until he reaches the teens, when criticism of parents usually reaches its peak.

How should feelings be expressed?

Restricting the child will not put a stop to his critical attitude toward his parents, though it will generally end his outspoken disapproval. What usually happens under such conditions is that the child develops a resentful attitude toward his parents and gives vent to his feelings about them behind their backs. Certainly, this is no way to encourage love and respect for parents or a good parent-child relationship!

Children's ideal of "mother"

EVERY child builds up an ideal of "Mother" by which he judges his own mother. This ideal is based in part on what his own mother is, what the mothers of his friends are, and on the mothers of fiction and poetry. Because your child will judge you according to his ideal, the more closely you approach this ideal, the greater will be his love and respect for you, and the more willing he will be to follow your guidance.

How children judge mother

A number of studies have been made of what American boys and girls think a mother should be. Here are some of the qualities they rank as "musts" for a mother. Why not look at yourself critically and see how you rate in these qualities:

1. *Personal Attractiveness.* A mother does not have to be beautiful, but all children like their mother to make a good appearance. This means good grooming, well-chosen clothes, a becoming hair style, and a cheerful friendliness.

2. *Youthfulness.* No child likes to have his mother mistaken for some elderly relative. To approach the child's ideal, the mother should guard against dowdiness. She need not follow the latest fashion fad, but she should dress with an eye to fashion and the style that suites her best. Going to an extreme in youthfulness is as bad as looking too old. A child quickly senses that his friends scoff at a mother who is trying to make people think she is his older sister, and this embarrasses him.

Youth vs. age

3. *Dignity.* Being silly and trying hard to be the life of the party is all right for other children, but when it comes to their own mother, it is a different story. Children like to look up to the person they call "Mother" and they cannot do so when she brings herself down to the level, in her speech and actions, of their own age.

4. *Understanding.* A child has many problems to meet and solve in life. To do this successfully, he must have the understanding and help of someone who is wiser and more experienced to guide him. If his mother doesn't understand how he feels about things that trouble him, how can she help him to solve his problems?

Troubles need to be shared

5. *Sympathy.* With true understanding comes sympathy. A child feels deeply, and he wants someone to share his feelings with him. Who can do this better than his mother? When he is hurt, either physically or emotionally, he wants to feel that he can turn to her for comfort and sympathy. Only under such conditions can a child feel secure in his home.

6. *Fairness.* A child likes to feel that his mother is perfectly fair to each and every member of the family. Even when *he* comes out ahead, he resents her unfairness to a brother or sister. No matter how strict she is, when a mother is fair, her children love and respect her in a way they could never love or respect a mother who played favorites.

7. *Tolerance.* A child likes to feel that the person whom he loves understands his faults and is tolerant of his shortcomings. When his school grades are poor or when he does not come up to his parents' expectations, Mother, he feels, should understand and forgive, and never hold a grudge against him.

Faults need to be forgiven

8. *Cheerfulness.* Nothing is more important to a child than being with a cheerful, happy person. No matter what happens, he looks to his mother to supply this emotional warmth. When a mother is depressed, and out of sorts, it quickly reflects on the child and makes him unhappy and depressed, too.

9. *Good Sportsmanship.* Mother should be a good sport if she wants her children to be. How can she expect them to be good losers in games, or cheerful when their favorite toys are broken, if she herself makes issues of trivial matters?

Playmates' opinions are important

10. *Popularity with Friends.* A child wants to know that his mother welcomes his friends and that his friends like to come to his house and like and respect his mother. This is especially important when a child reaches school age and his playmates become an important influence in his life. It helps build up his trust in his mother and his feeling of security in his own place in his home and family.

Someone to turn to

11. *Helpfulness.* The mother who is ever ready to help the child when he needs help comes close to his ideal. When things are going his way and he can manage for himself, he does not turn to his mother for help. But just knowing that she is there and ready to help him when he needs her help is important to him.

12. *Achievements.* A child who can boast to his friends that "My mother bakes the best cakes you have ever eaten," or that she has some other excellence, feels that he has an extra feather in his own cap. He wants his mother to be important to others and, when she is, she seems more important to him.

Home comes first

13. *Always Available.* This does not mean that a child necessarily resents a working mother. It does mean that he wants to know that his mother is there when he needs her. Knowing that mother will be home when he returns from school or play is important to a child. But if she works, knowing he can reach her by telephone will also reassure him. For what he really wants to know is that he is important to her and that she loves and enjoys her home and family.

Children's ideal of "father"

Because fathers of today must be away from home more than fathers of the past, when much of their work was carried on in or near the home, a father's relationship with his children is more limited. However, it is the quality rather than the quantity of the time spent with the children that counts. As is true of mothers, children have definite ideals of what a father should be. Fathers, unfortunately, fall short of these ideals more than mothers. There are two reasons for this: fathers are less conscious of what the role of a father should be, and most fathers tend to expect more of their children than the children are capable of. Then they become disappointed or disgusted with the child—an attitude the child quickly senses and resents.

Qualities of an ideal father

As with mothers, studies have been made of what children want their fathers to be like and what qualities they would like their fathers to possess. How do you, as a father, rate yourself on the following qualities?

1. *Youthful Appearance.* A child does not want his father to look like a teen-ager, but he doesn't want him mistaken for his grandfather either. To help make your child proud of your appearance—and in behalf of your own good health—keep yourself as physically trim as possible. Add good grooming and a cheery smile and your child will point to his father with pride.

Father's place in the world

2. *Achievement.* Not all achievement is measured by material success or social prestige. To a child his father is a success, no matter what work he does, as long as he has the respect of people around him, and the child can trust in his integrity and honesty. Even small children observe more than we think they do and are quick to compare what you say with what you do. It is important for a child to have faith in his father's values, for he often models his own behavior on them.

Will father understand?

3. *Understanding.* A child often turns to his father for special understanding since he is not involved in the small mishaps of the day as the mother is. A father can create a close bond with his child if he responds to this appeal wisely, and his special man's viewpoint can help both his sons and his daughters.

4. *Tolerance.* A child hopes his father will be tolerant of his shortcomings, for this will bolster the child's faith in his own ability to overcome them. A wise father will make an effort to be patient and to guide his child gently along the road to maturity. He will find his reward in his child's love, loyalty, and trust.

5. *Willingness to do things with child.* Because the mother is usually ready and willing to do things with and for the child, it is natural for the child to expect the same of his father. In the case of boys especially, the desire to have their father as a playmate and companion is strong, particularly when they reach school age and find that their friends' fathers are their chums and playmates. How do you rate here in the eyes of your child?

6. *Fairness.* Because, traditionally, the father is the family disciplinarian, the child has a good opportunity to judge how fair or unfair he is. When you punish or scold your child, do you find out first what prompted the act you believe deserves punishment, or do you judge the behavior according to adult standards? Are you fair in your punishments when you let out your pent-up anger for something that went wrong in business by being more severe than your child's behavior justifies?

7. *Reasonable Expectations.* Far too many fathers expect their children to do things way beyond the child's capacities. When they are successful men, or when they are failures and have never achieved what they wanted from the time they were children, they are likely to set their goals too high for their children and then be bitterly disappointed when their children do not reach these goals. How can a child love and respect a father who is disappointed in him?

Your role as parent

I KNOW that adults find it difficult to change the pattern of their lives and adjust to new situations as easily as they did when they were younger. Still, *it is important that they try to adjust to the pattern of a good parent.* Once they take on the responsibilities of parenthood, it is up to them to play this role as successfully as they can. This means many sacrifices of personal interests and pleasures, not only for the mother but for the father as well. No longer can they hope to have the carefree days of their courtship or early marriage. They are now parents and should act as parents.

To be a good parent may mean definite changes in attitudes and behavior. Having spent many years learning to put away childish things and developing more mature interests, parents are now faced with the problem of going back to their own childhood years and remembering how they felt and acted in situations like those their children now face. They must try to see life through childish eyes, just as they did when they were children. This is not easy for mature men and women, and they often fall short in this respect.

And yet, without this ability, how can parents understand their children and give them the understanding and help they need? How can they be tolerant of childish weaknesses and mistakes, and how can they be real pals to their children? This does not mean going back to second childhood; but it does mean developing the dual personality pattern of a child and an adult. Because every child expects his parents to act their ages, a parent cannot come down to the child's level and *stay* there. *He must learn to shift back and forth as circumstances require and as his children's needs change.*

When I was young

My husband is always saying to our children, "When I was young ..."
This irritates them and makes them stubborn. Am I right in
telling my husband that he should not harp on his youth?

You certainly are right in your advice to your husband. Times have changed; when your husband was a boy, things were very different from what they are now. He cannot, therefore, compare *his* childhood with that of his children. The psychological effect of beginning his remarks to your children with, "When I was young, etc.," is to make them think he is thinking of *himself* and not of them. In short, it creates the impression that he does not have enough interest in them to try to understand *them* and *their* problems. Children are self-centered enough to want attention to be focused on *themselves* and on their own affairs. Your husband's constant reference to his own youth runs counter to this desire.

Allow criticism

My son Tom, who is 8 years old, has started to criticize
his father and me rudely. My husband gets very
angry and has taken to washing the boy's mouth out with soap.
I get angry, too, but so far I have not punished him
though I scold him severely. How should we handle this problem?

I question whether the way either you or your husband are handling your son's criticisms is good. Certainly an 8-year-old boy is too old to have his mouth washed out. Your Tom will merely become resentful of such treatment and will not realize why his criticisms of his parents are wrong. Scolding, which is your way of handling the matter, will not correct the faults either, because you are not showing Tom *why* criticisms of the sort he makes are rude and disrespectful.

Instead of using the tactics you and your husband have used till now, why not ask Tom to talk frankly with you—in a polite manner, of course—and explain what he does not like about what you do or say? Tell him you are always glad to have his point of view, but that giving it rudely is not the way to do it. Listen to what he has to say. He might have a point of view quite different from yours or your husband's because he sees the matter through a child's eyes, not through the eyes of an adult.

In the future, you and your husband should be careful of the way *you* criticize Tom. If *you* bark at him or say unpleasant things in an unpleasant manner, you are setting a pattern that *he* is bound to follow when he criticizes you. You should be as respectful and kindly in your criticisms of Tom's behavior as you expect him to be of yours.

Lack of interest

> *My husband is a very busy man and works hard. However, I feel that he should devote some time to the children in the evenings and over week-ends. He says this is my work and that he has enough to do with his business. The children feel badly about his lack of interest and are becoming very critical of their father.*

Because so many fathers today show a genuine interest in their children, your children are noticing the difference between the way their father treats them and the way their friends' fathers act. Naturally this comparison is unfavorable to your husband. His neglect of his children is unfair to himself and to the children. Your husband is not only shirking his parental responsibilities but he is also missing out on a lot of fun he could have with the children.

Can you not make him see this? Point out to him that a father's responsibility is not limited to keeping a roof over his children's heads, and putting food into their mouths. It also includes helping them to develop into the type of men and women he would want them to be. Try to arrange picnics, family trips to movies and other places of amusement, and pleasant family gatherings before the television with refreshments. In this way, your husband will get to know his children better and they will see him as a companion instead of a disciplinarian. This may help to bring your children and your husband closer together and arouse his real interest in them.

Overworked

How can a busy mother be a good mother to her children?
I have six children and no help. I am so busy with the housework that
I never have time to do anything with or for the children
except take care of their physical needs. I realize
I am depriving them of many of the things a mother should do.

You are right: you are depriving your children of the most important things a mother can give her children. *Of course* it is important to feed, clothe, and take care of their bodily needs. But what about the mental side of their development? They need the stimulation you can give them and they need the example you can set for them to follow.

Try to systematize your work so that you will not have your nose to the grindstone all the time. Cut corners whenever possible. Have your older children help you with many of the household tasks to free you to do things for and with the children. It is not so much the quantity of time you spend with them that counts as the quality. If you give them your undivided attention for 15 minutes when you are doing things with them, or when you are discussing their problems, that will mean more to them than 30 minutes during which they feel you are distracted by something else.

You can, of course, carry on certain routine jobs in the home, such as ironing, while talking to the children or telling them stories. When you set them to work on household tasks, why not do your work in the same room with them, so you can all talk together and have a sociable time? This will make the work pleasanter for all concerned and will give you more time to be with your children.

Grade-conscious husband

My husband is very much interested in the children's grades,
but he shows no interest in what they are studying or doing in school.
I feel that this is a bad emphasis and encourages
the children to be too grade-conscious.

You are right. Putting so much weight on grades as your husband does not only puts the wrong emphasis on school work, but also encourages children to cheat so that their grades will come up to parental expectations. Try to arouse in your husband a sincere interest in all aspects of your children's school life—their teachers, their friends, their school activities. Have him attend the Parent-Teacher Association meetings with you and discuss with the children what they do in school every day. If he could hear their lessons or help them when they need some further explanation of their work, the children would have an entirely different feeling about their father's attitude toward their schooling.

Intolerance

My mother lives with us. She was very anxious for me to have children but now that I have three, she complains that they get on her nerves and she is very impatient with them. She had a big family of her own and that should make her more understanding and tolerant of her grandchildren.

YOUR mother was younger when her own family was growing up. Probably it was easier for her to be patient then. As people grow older, they tire more quickly, and it is harder for them to stand the noise and bustle all normal children create. Try to give your mother some quiet, rest periods each day and don't ask her to do much baby-sitting. Try, too, to help the children understand why she is impatient with them. If they make a special effort to be considerate of her, she probably will be much more patient with them.

Parents' attitudes

I have been married recently and am planning to give up my work as my husband is very anxious to have a family. I honestly do not like little children and I am wondering if I will make a good mother.

A GOOD mother must like children. Are you sure that your dislike for children is not due to the fact that you have had little contact with them and that you hate to give up your work with the financial independence it gives you and the pleasant contacts outside the home? Before you have a child, try to determine in your own mind if you cannot become a good mother if you are willing to try. Take advantage of every possible opportunity to be with friends who have children and observe their manner of handling them. Study some books on child care and development and attend any lectures on the subject offered in your community. All of this will help you to become interested in children and to develop an understanding of them; this is essential to successful motherhood.

Index

Guide to questions and answers

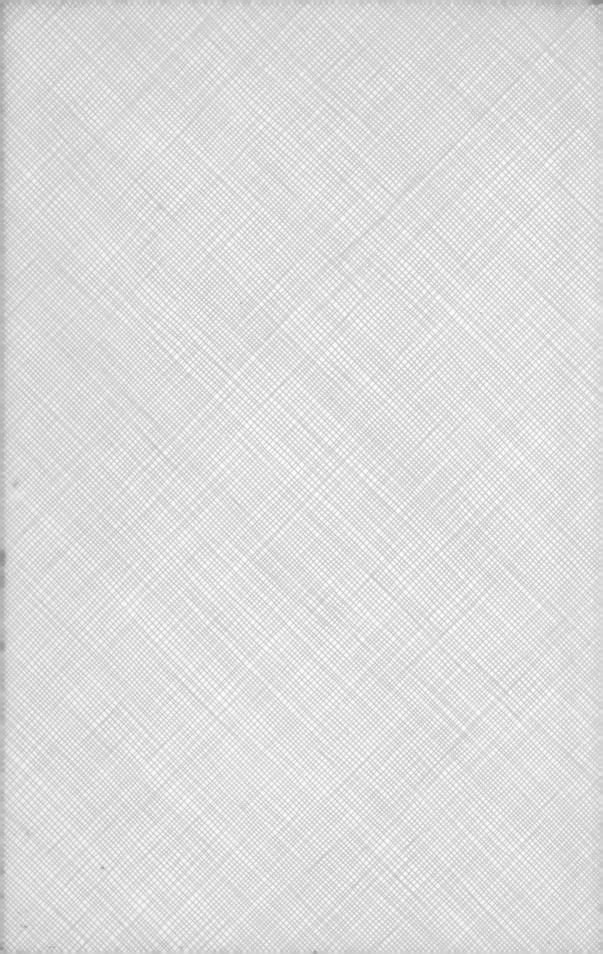